W9-ASA-301

SAINT BENEDICT
ON THE FREEWAY

SAINT BENEDICT ON THE FREEWAY

🌹 A Rule of Life
for the 21st Century

Corinne Ware

Abingdon Press
Nashville

SAINT BENEDICT ON THE FREEWAY
A RULE OF LIFE FOR THE 21st CENTURY

Copyright © 2001 by Abingdon Press

All rights reserved.
No part of this work may be reproduced (except as noted below) or transmitted in any form or by any means, electronic or mechanical, including photocopying and recording, or by any information storage or retrieval system, except as may be expressly permitted by the 1976 Copyright Act or in writing from the publisher. Requests for permission should be addressed to Abingdon Press, P.O. Box 801, 201 Eighth Avenue South, Nashville, TN 37202-0801.

This book is printed on recycled, acid-free, elemental-chlorine–free paper.

Library of Congress Cataloging-in-Publication Data

Ware, Corinne.
    Saint Benedict on the freeway : a rule of life for the 21st century / Corinne Ware.
        p. cm.
    Includes bibliographical references.
    ISBN 0-687-04610-6 (alk. paper)
        1. Benedict, Saint, Abbot of Monte Cassino. Regula. 2. Spiritual life—Christianity. I. Title.

    BX3004.Z5 W36 2001
    255'.106—dc21

                                                                                    2001046366

The publisher grants permission for copying and distribution of page 77 and pages 129-34 for educational purposes only.

Scripture quotations not otherwise marked are taken from the *New Revised Standard Version of the Bible,* © copyright 1989, Division of Christian Education of the National Council of the Churches of Christ in the United States of America. Used by permission. All rights reserved.

Scripture noted NASB taken from the NEW AMERICAN STANDARD BIBLE®, © Copyright The Lockman Foundation 1960, 1962, 1963, 1968, 1971, 1972, 1973, 1975, 1977, 1995. Used by permission.

Scripture quotations marked (NIV) are taken from the HOLY BIBLE, NEW INTERNATIONAL VERSION®. NIV®. Copyright © 1973, 1978, 1984 by International Bible Society. Used by permission of Zondervan Publishing House. All rights reserved.

Scripture quotations marked (RSV) are taken from the *Revised Standard Version of the Bible,* copyright 1946, 1952, 1971 by the Division of Christian Education of the National Council of the Churches of Christ in the United States of America. Used by permission. All rights reserved.

Scripture quotations marked KJV are taken from the King James or Authorized Version of the Bible.

Excerpt from "Choruses from The Rock" in COLLECTED POEMS 1909–1962 by T. S. Eliot, copyright 1936 by Harcourt, Inc., copyright © 1964, 1963 by T. S. Eliot, reprinted by permission of the publisher.

From BEING HOME by Gunilla Norris, copyright © 1991 by Gunilla Norris. Used by permission of Bell Tower, a division of Random House, Inc.

Scripture noted *The Message* taken from *THE MESSAGE.* Copyright © Eugene H. Peterson, 1993, 1994, 1995. Used by permission of NavPress Publishing Group.

01 02 03 04 05 06 07 08 09 10 — 10 9 8 7 6 5 4 3 2 1

MANUFACTURED IN THE UNITED STATES OF AMERICA

In Tribute
Mollie, Eleanor, Liz, and Jody

While we were standing together at the back of the basilica, there was suddenly a tremendous gust of wings. Sparrows and pigeons were continually flying around, but this gust of wings was mighty and different. We looked up, and there, high above the narthex was the unmistakable, compelling face of a barn owl. Again and again, it flew and paused, frantically crashing its white body with terrible hopelessness against the dusty windows. Every so often it would fly the whole length of the church, only to soar up again into another barrier of light. I cannot describe how unbearable it was to follow the flight of that bird, knowing that we were quite incapable to give it its freedom. There were holes and spaces, if only it would see them. Each time it failed, the pause and the stillness became longer, and the fearful despair of the bird felt greater.

We left. . . . We couldn't bear to be there. Later, the whole experience haunted me. The gaze of that particular bird is so involving. I suddenly thought, what if God witnesses in every man a divine spark, which flies within us blindly, like that bird, crashing in terror, punched and pounded from wall to wall, blinded by obstacles and dust, and yet, God knows, that there is a way for natural freedom and ascending flight. What an extraordinary pain that witness would be.

—Jennifer Lash
On Pilgrimage

❧❧ Contents

✼ Foreword

We live in a new period of spiritual awakening, in the midst of a fast-paced, rapidly changing, pluralistic culture. Every historical spiritual awakening seems marked by a sense of both need and possibility for a fuller personal and communal relationship with the divine. The current awakening is no exception. A major strand of this new awakening involves the desire for a greater interiorization of spiritual reality that takes into account the unique movements of God's Spirit in our daily lives.

It has been said that in recent decades we have been moving from the experience of authority to the authority of experience. More people are giving value to their own spiritual experience, and seeing the value of historical and contemporary religious authorities primarily in terms of how they can assist us to recognize the presence and unique whispers of God in our personal lives and in the lives of the various levels of community to which we belong.

Many people in their hearts have rejected the kind of religious authority that interprets spiritual truth as objective rational beliefs and behaviors that are to be blindly imposed on our lives, disregarding the unique situations of people. Instead, this strand of the modern awakening gives emphasis to the living, free Spirit of God that is forever creating fresh possibilities in the unique circumstances of our lives and inviting us to deeper communion and compassion through our response to these God-given openings. God is seen as an intimate, loving, insistent presence in and among us, not as a far-off judge and ruler. Weight is given to our being made in the image of God (Genesis 1:27), and to our individual and corporate spiritual journeys as distinctive, evolving ways of living from that Spirit-inspired divine image.

This understanding gives enormous dignity to each person's

life, because God's Spirit is trusted to live through that life in hidden and visible ways. These ways are marred by our sad willfulness and lack of recognition of who we and others really are: the beloved community of the living God. This is far from a privatistic American individualism, because it recognizes that we belong intimately together and to all of God's creation. But it does recognize the need to attend to God's Spirit within us in order to live out our part of the kin-dom of God.

I believe this valuable new book of Corinne Ware's is a very helpful, practical expression of this dimension of our modern spiritual awakening. She carefully recognizes the cultural situation of the people for whom she writes, a situation marked by life on the run, lived on the surface, and yearning for more of God. In the midst of this situation she singles out a particular need: how to be present to God through all the hours of the day, and not just at special times. Historically, one way of expressing this need is, "How can I practice the presence of God through all that happens in my life?" This is particularly difficult to do in the kind of fragmented, fragmenting, pressured, ever-changing daily life that is so common today. She rightly senses that we need to have, as I would word it, a strong desire for givenness to God through our daily living, if practicing the presence really is going to happen.

She chooses the historic Benedictine Rule of life as both a symbol and in its essence a practical help for modern people who are moved to dispose themselves to a more steady presence to the larger Presence in which life is unfolding moment by moment. She sees that Rule as offering concrete ways to remember God through the thoughts and activities of our day. She doesn't restrict herself to that Rule, though, in offering many practical ways to attend God's presence through the day.

She insightfully orients the value of spiritual disciplines to their capacity to help us be more constantly conscious of God in what we are already doing in daily life. We could say that our disciplines then don't add something to what we are doing. Rather, they help remind us of our desire for God through whatever we are doing, and our trust in God's involvement in every moment. Such an awareness has a way of opening us more responsively to the One who is alive in and through us in all situations of our daily lives.

The Study Guide for each chapter makes this an ideal book for small group study, as well as for individual understanding. Overall, the book provides a fine introduction to a wide range of spiritual disciplines, with special weight on the contributions of the Benedictine Rule adapted for modern daily life. Adopting some of these practices, as they are right for our particular lives, can help us live in the divine eye of our tumultuous daily hurricane.

TILDEN EDWARDS

Acknowledgments

There is a liturgical phrase that is sometimes said following the public reading of scripture: *Thanks be to God.* I do thank God for help given me through friends and colleagues who have wanted to make this book as clear and helpful as it could be. I owe much to the two outstanding librarians who work in the Booher Library at the Episcopal Theological Seminary of the Southwest in Austin, Texas. Makail McIntosh-Doty went through my manuscript with a sympathetic eye, weeding out commas and giving encouragement. Director of the Library, Rob Cogswell, made invaluable suggestions as to sequence and placement. Both of them always "believed" in the book.

This is my first time to publish with Abingdon Press and it has been a pleasant and supportive experience. My thanks to Ezra Earl Jones, formerly General Secretary of the General Board of Discipleship, The United Methodist Church, for opening the Abingdon door. To all those at Abingdon who work at getting a book to market, I say my thanks.

The four names which appear on the dedication page are women who have been my close friends for fifty years. Thanks be to God.

🙢 Introduction

*We yearn for something primordial at the center of our
soul, something from our spiritual history which, like a
guiding star in the sky two millennia ago, might illuminate
a better way.*

—Robert E. Cogswell
Religion: Choosing What We Think

Years ago Peggy Lee sang the line, "Is that all there is?" The
song's plaintive query forms the underlying theme of questions we now ask ourselves, questions that became louder as
we exited one century to enter another. Those of us in the West
are aware of a certain lack of depth in our fast-forward lives,
full as they are of all that we had hoped would make us happy.
We wonder if, indeed, this is all that there is. How many writers, do you suppose, currently use the phrase "search for
meaning" in books, articles, speeches, and sermons? The
phrase recurs because it cries out a yearning to heal the rift felt
between our daily life and the sacred. Michael Lindsay, Gallup
consultant for religion and culture, reports that he sees a clear
trend toward people wanting to explore their faith.

Often we search for this meaning by changing the course of
our religious life. In the past decade 30 to 40 percent of
Americans have switched denominations or faith groups.[1] We
cast aside the traditional in favor of a customized, a la carte
faith and a more personalized spirituality. A hyperdrive life
demands instant gratification and a not too difficult formula
for spirituality. Having investigated outer space during the
past century, we now turn our attention to the exploration of
inner space as we begin the new one. The central question
becomes, how will we live a life capable of hearing the "still
small voice" of God, while experiencing the speed and sensory

overload of modern life? How does one hear God's voice in the twenty-first century?

Life Lived on the Surface

Jesus told a story about a person who wanted to plant seed so that a crop would grow. As was the custom of the day, the sower cast the seed about by hand with some landing on hard ground, some on rocky, some in thorny places, and a few dropping in fertile soil. This is often called the Parable of the Sower and is told by Jesus in the New Testament in Matthew, chapter 13. The secret to the parable's meaning is thought to be the comparison of the various soils to various types of people. The reader thinks of God, or perhaps Jesus, as the sower of the seed, the seed as being God's word, and us as the soils onto which that word, or seed, is sown. The general response, on hearing the story, is to identify immediately for ourselves just who is the hard, roadside soil; who is the rocky or thorny ground (those who will not respond to God), and who is the good soil. We would so much rather think of ourselves as the good soil, with the less productive ground being somebody else, "the others." But what if each individual person is, within themselves, all of the soils?[2]

If I were to think of myself as having within me all the varieties of soils, in other words, of manifesting each of these varied responses to God, how then would I see myself as the subject of this parable? Matthew, who relates the story, goes on to say that Jesus later makes some comparisons, helping his followers to decipher his meaning. The reason the hard ground, the rocky ground, and the ground filled with thorns do not produce a crop is because, although the seed (the word from God) is spread on them, other influences are so overpowering that the seed will not root and grow. Either the seed is snatched away, possibly by birds, or it is burned by the sun. It may take root for awhile, but when the root is crowded out by rocks, it withers. And hardy thorns are too much competition for a tender new plant. If I am all these soils, might it be that my attention to God is dissipated by the encroaching distractions of my outwardly focused life? How can God's still small voice, which is the seed in the story, get a hearing if all the other voices are so much louder? If I am unable to make the God-connection, I may go on leading my supposedly full life asking all the while, "Is that all there is?"

Life on the Run

Our lives are lived at top speed. Advertisements entice us to buy cars that are faster and more exciting than the one we are now driving. We complain that flying is not speedy enough because of the airport wait. Once in the terminal, we get on a cell phone so we can ratchet things up a bit further. We e-mail instead of sending "snail mail," watch cable television and get live, real-time coverage from everywhere in the world. In our addiction to urgency, we reach for palm-sized computers which enable us to do our business at an even more accelerated pace as we push farther into the new century.

None of this is bad; none of it is evil. In fact, all the convenience is very helpful if what we need is to communicate and get on with an efficient life. But it *is* distracting! "The birds of the air have eaten up the sown word," says one writer, "the thorns of everyday life have choked it; all that remains of it is a vague regret in the soul."[3] Our distractions translate into a life lived on the surface. Energies spent in crisis management translate into stressed bodies and distorted values. However, we suspect that speed and busyness are not all there is. Being able to connect by fax and phone and modem seems somehow not to enhance the God-connection. So there must be some other way to make this deeper union.

Trend Toward the Transcendent

People say there's good news and there's bad news. Actually, there is good news and there is promising news. The good news is what is happening among those who want the "something more." During the 1980s and 1990s that closed the twentieth century, we became less content to live our days only on the surface, allowing external static (the rocks and thorns) to block internal growth and inner quiet. Never before have we had so many books on spirituality, so many growth seminars, retreat centers, and spiritual enrichment programs. Not that all of it is helpful, or even good, but we are, nonetheless, trying to find the "more." Spirituality has become religiously correct.

You may have noticed the resurgence, even among Protestant Christians, of what is called spiritual direction, the one-on-one encounter between one who is mature in faith and one who wants to be companioned in the spiritual search. In response to pressure from laypersons and theological students, seminaries scramble to add spiritual formation courses to their already crowded curriculum offerings. The sale of religious books has increased dramatically. Retreat centers were once difficult to find, even if you were willing to drive long distances. Today you can locate one or several close by, and more are to come. Retreat experiences, such as Cursillo and Walk to Emmaus, as well as walking the labyrinth—a large mandala-on-the-floor—are sought by thousands of Christians and inquirers. Taizé, a singing form of worship that originated in a Protestant monastic community in the south of France, grows in popularity each year. Churches in many denominations now offer Taizé's liturgical format as an alternative service of worship, especially for young members. By many paths and byways, the religious and nonreligious are trying very hard to find the center in an off-center society.

Something More

So the good news is that many of the religious and spiritual efforts we now make richly contribute to our lives. Question anyone on the spiritual journey, and they are likely to tell you that some particular event was the turning point in their lives. These events are what one author calls "watershed times," and writes that at such times "we know that we live our way deeply in the present, only to discover that we are invaded by the

18

Eternal."[4] *What is lacking, it appears, is a continuous, daily consciousness of God versus momentary inspirations.* Seekers after a deeper spiritual life often plan their schedules around those opportunities that allow them to get away for spiritual refreshment. But many wish their lives could be God-connected all the time, during every day, and that the religious experience could be maintained in the "between times." The German friar Meister Eckhart observed that "whoever seeks God in some special Way, will gain the Way and lose God who is hidden in the Way. But whoever seeks God without any special Way, finds Him as He really is."[5] Eckhart believed that God was most readily found in the common, the daily.

Years ago I taped on my refrigerator door the cartoon of a maid, mop in hand, saying to her astonished employer, "I'm leaving because life around here is just so daily!" The maid wanted more days that were special. We yearn for an experience of the transcendent that is more than occasional. In this instance I believe that the language of *transformation* is appropriate. Rather than simply being influenced with momentary grace, we want to be deeply and lastingly transformed! We would like very much to experience the inner center, the at-peacefulness that we suspect is possible, and that we sometimes, though rarely, glimpse in our contemporaries.

Poet and author Diane Ackerman has written a book titled *Deep Play.*[6] It's about being entirely at home in the present and in common events, about enjoying every moment for what it is. Good self-help advice, but what would foster such a feeling? I have concluded that such an experience is possible only when we are comfortable being in creation and when we feel connected to its Creator. In fact, we feel best when we are actively helping with creation, when we are "in sync" with God, so to speak, and cocreators with God. Along with John Wesley, I think we want not just to have devotional time, but a devotional life. Going further back than Wesley, we see the sixth-century monk, St. Benedict, wrestling with how he might craft this sort of deeply connected and purposeful life. It is from him that we hope to learn things that will translate into our own time. Before we engage Benedict, however, we will consider alternate approaches which may parallel and add color to our appreciation of his approach.

New Time, a New Century

Addressing the subject of changing attitudes toward spirituality, the editorial in a recent theological journal warns that "it is too late to put the genie back in the bottle." The editor comments on "the bewildering abundance of spiritual offerings," and says with amazement that "Baptists read Maximus the Confessor, Catholics read Jonathan Edwards, [and] Dutch Calvinists read John of the Cross."[7] Another editor notes that "Our world today is Post-Freudian, Post-Modern, Post Christian, Post Rationalist, Post Newtonian, [and] practically Post Millennial," by which he means we've "been there; done that."[8] During the past century we hitched our stars to political and social reform, to portfolio statements and graduate degrees, and occasionally even to high religious moments. With so much already tried, we wonder, "Is that all there is?" We suspect there is something more. And, indeed there is. The task of transformation is to find a way to keep the Sower's holy seed alive and continuously growing in us, to see that it takes deep root in the good soil of our open spirits.

But first, we must figure out what such a life would look like. There is no twenty-first century model out there, awaiting our inspection. There are patterns from the past, however, created by those who have wondered the same things we are wondering now and have, in their own centuries, crafted for themselves ways to maintain spiritual connectedness. I believe that we too are able to craft ways of being God-connected in our daily lives, even though we live in a century that seems not to support such an effort.

A Plan for Awareness

What is ahead is a plan for becoming aware, daily, of the presence of God. Chapter 1 calls this awareness being "recollected," a term used in the past to describe the gathering up of one's attention toward God. The question asked is whether recollection can be practiced today within a culture of distraction. We will also look into the aspirations and yearnings of other religious faiths, all of which seek the "something more." What is the common thread among them, the clue that will tell us what is necessary in order to find God in our own time and place?

Chapter 2 presents an ancient monastic practice called "The Rule" and examines why some practices fail while others succeed. The question asked is whether there is anything at all in the ancient Rule of Life that would inform us in the twenty-first century. Looking at these life patterns, what can we use that will enhance our own lives? Is a Rule of Life burdensome, compulsive, and perhaps impossible in our time, or can it be made liberating and life giving?

Chapters 3 and 4 offer the reader ways to translate into our own accelerated times approaches which once served the needs of those living in a very different society and period of history. Chapter 3 looks at "the Hours," a pattern of punctuations in the day designed as prayerful pauses. Unlike the monks, we do not seek to live in cloistered communities, stopping our work for an hour at a time as we pray together, but if we are creative, we can reinterpret "the Hours" to our own uses. Chapter 4 continues the emphasis on the sacramental day by noticing those things, common and daily, that ground us in the spiritual life that is around us. These are the "triggers" that help us to associate what we see with listening to the still small voice of God.

Most of us pray in some way or other. We usually think of "saying prayers" as the way to communicate with God. Chapter 5 lays before the reader several of the many ways in which one may enter into this holy conversation. All of life, in fact, can become prayer if we are attentive to God's presence in the world and in ourselves.

Chapter 6 concludes by drawing together the ideas needed to create for ourselves a Rule of Life that can be designed to work in the twenty-first century.

As much as we may need high moments of spiritual

transcendence and revelation, we need also the matrix of a daily discipline holding us and supporting us in the continuous awareness of God. Occasional times of great inspiration can spur us on, but it is in daily living that we learn to sustain growth and find the "something more." This is a book for cultivation of the holy in the "between times." It is here that we till the fertile ground in which the seed that is sown within us may flourish.

CHAPTER ONE

Collected and Recollected

You are the topos tou theou *(God's place) and the spiritual life is nothing more or less than to allow that space to exist where God can dwell, to create a space where his glory can manifest itself.*
                                                    —John Eudes Bamberger

"I just have to stop and *collect* myself!" she says. "Everything's happening at once and I'm about to come apart." Down the hallway an executive cradles his head in his hands and moans, "This pressure is getting to me." Events crash in relentlessly and we experience the panicky despair common to us all, that feeling of being scattered, fragmented, and uncentered. It is more typical than not, in this century of acceleration, that we will be confronted by decisions before we have even had a chance to think through what we need to do. Few of us enjoy the luxury of "enough time." There are periods when we feel unprepared for even the expected and for what we have known all along was about to happen. We have days and months when it seems that everyone and everything makes demands on us at the same moment. Pressure builds and what we may want most in the world is a closet in which to hide, a stretch of wave-washed beach where we can forget it all, a person who will give us that soothing promise that things will be all right again. We want anything that will lift us out of our dilemmas. If only we might have just a moment to collect ourselves.

Times like these illustrate—indeed, prove to us—that we believe ourselves to be happy or unhappy as a result of circumstance.

Isn't it true, after all, that if things go well we will be happy? I think we must admit that it does help. Who among us can realistically say that circumstance, good or bad, does not affect us? It is more than reasonable that we should make efforts to secure for ourselves and those we love safety, security, comfort, and advantage. The person who does not strive to secure these blessings is usually called impractical and, at worst, masochistic.

Singer Sophie Tucker told us, "I've been rich and I've been poor, and rich is better." Although we've seen that this is not true in every case, nevertheless, circumstances do matter. It helps to have resources! In asking the question, "Is that all there is?" we are actually wondering out loud about resources. What or whom may we call upon to get us through the times when circumstances are against us? And even when life seems to be cloudless and our circumstances quite good, where is that enjoyment and tranquility we expected to experience? It is a commonplace that we suffer that vacant dis-ease that comes when one is vaguely unhappy even though things are going well. We want to know, "If everything is so good, why do I feel so bad?" It is our "not at home in the world" feeling.

What Is Recollection?

The frantic plaint, "I just have to get myself collected," is exactly opposite from the calm assertion "I am recollected." *Recollection* is a word used by spiritual writers, mostly in the past, who wanted to describe *the concentration of the attention on the presence of God*. It is sometimes used in a more limited way to describe a particular stage of prayer during which someone is so stilled that God may work in that person without hindrance. For our purposes, the first and more general definition is the more helpful. Being recollected simply means being conscious that God is with you. The essential feeling is that of being *accompanied*. It suggests the development of an interior life within a person, one that is not the same as exterior and circumstantial events, but which nonetheless affects every aspect of one's life. All of this has to do with what we are currently calling "spirituality," a term that is often used and seldom defined. Geoffrey Wainwright defines spirituality as the "combination of praying and living."[1] The inner life of recollection inevitably results in an increased outer life of connection, compassion, and a certain composure.

Recollection, as it once was called, is a mental state of awareness. It serves as the connective tissue that holds all our life within the matrix of a consciousness of God. For instance, the religious but unrecollected person (most of us) may attend services of worship, act according to a religion-based ethic in the conduct of work and relationships, give money to charitable causes, and even say formal prayers at specific times. All of this is extremely commendable and, indeed, such acts are part of the very fabric of civil society and provide some personal fulfillment. But there is something important to notice about this. In fulfilling these obligations, we may be segregating our acts from our thoughts and attitudes at those times when we are not especially engaging in "religious" things. Very often we participate in religious activities as special events disconnected from the rest of life. Acts we do in obedience to our highest values are good things, and they enrich our lives and the lives of others. Scripture says such conduct "pleases God." That is no guarantee, however, that we will feel God's presence within us, long term. The "something more" that we seek is that sense of always being accompanied, of God-with-us at all times and not in special moments only.

Theologian Paul Tillich writes about "ecstatic reasoning," by which he means the intersection of the immediate with the ultimate, the horizontal with the vertical.[2] In other words, what is going on right now can be informed and influenced by my consciousness that God is also "going on" right now. Whatever is happening in the present moment, God is also happening, which is to say, God is active. It is as though we learn to think of two things in tandem—our experience of the events of the moment and our experience of God in the moment. This concept is actually not a foreign one. You can recall times in your life when you have heard in your mind the inner voice of a parent or teacher just as you were about to speak or act. You were thinking of both the immediate circumstance and of the inner voice all at once. Take a moment to remember times when this sort of tandem thinking made a difference in what you did or did not do.

These inner values can be good and important, but there is a potential problem for us if the voice we hear tears us down rather than builds us up. How easy and natural it is to resent the voices we do not like. Didn't they often deprive us of the very thing we wanted most at the time? We may even recall them as putting us down, not an uncommon experience for many. Seeing God as the parent who denies, or the stern and punitive teacher, we might even want God to go away!

Think instead of how you felt when you were deeply in love with someone, one who's presence in your thoughts accompanied and dominated all your waking moments. To think of the person you loved affirmed you and made you feel alive and whole. This is exactly how we experience a consciousness of the divine when we see God as God truly is. It takes a lot of unlearning for some of us to believe that God is "for us," that God wills our good in the moment, and at every moment. Theologians name this quality of God's being with us as God's *immanence*. The opposite experience of God would be to feel God as distant, remote, and uninvolved, even hostile. It is no wonder that we feel lonely if this is how we see the Creator. One who experiences God as remote interprets the Creator as being uninterested in the creation. An honest person would admit to feeling rejected and hurt by such a perception, and probably angry. This underlying sense of abandonment by God expresses itself in many ways. To relieve the isolation, we may seek constantly to be in the presence of other people, so as not to feel so alone, or we may claim not to care about God, if God exists at all. On the human level, we see ourselves use these same defenses when we feel rejected by people who are important to us.

All religions attempt to bring their adherents into some sort of harmony with the divine, a harmony which overcomes this empty feeling of separateness. Each may see God very differently, but the overwhelming common desire is to bridge what is perceived as the gap between the human and the divine.

The Common Quest of All Religions

Major religious traditions have as their ultimate goal the union of the creation with the Creator. Whether this union is a merging or a profound connection depends on how a religion views the capacities of human beings. Nevertheless, it is a moving toward God (or the Infinite) that characterizes most of the ascetic disciplines of major faith groups. As one author put it, there are "many paths to the same summit."[3] This is not to claim that all paths are of equal value or that all faith traditions are the same. For the purposes of this inquiry, those judgments are left to others.

A common ground in the major religions is the hunger to be in union with the one who creates. It is a quest for meaning and a desire to move beyond unsatisfying self-centeredness. The word religion *(religio)* actually means "rebinding." This yearning for union and transcendence is the motivating engine for the religious practices found in Christianity, Hinduism, Buddhism, Islam, Judaism, and many other religions. Although this book is not exclusively for the Christian reader, it is primarily addressed to the person who is largely formed by that tradition. To my fellow Christian, I would say that I find it affirming, not threatening, to realize that we are not the only ones seeking a sense of being accompanied by God. If other traditions seek what I am seeking, it encourages me to think that, as a human being, I am somehow on the right track, certainly in those areas on which there is common ground. It is encouraging to know that seeking a state of recollection, which is a continuous awareness of God, is not some quirkiness found just in me or only in Christianity, but is a fundamental human hunger.

When religions become too institutionalized, their followers are likely to forget their original purpose and so no longer remember that *connection* was the central reason for being. Religious services are meant to enable our worship of God and our experience of union with the Creator. They badly miss their mark when they become staged productions, instruments of recruitment, entertainment, or even something that must be done because it's a particular day. If I am honest, I will ask myself why I am going to a worship service at this particular time, and what I expect and hope for when I get there. I may expect to meet someone whose company I enjoy, or perhaps may just want to keep up my reputation as a churchgoer and a religious person. Seeing the person I wanted to meet and maintaining my reputation are not unworthy goals. The deprivation occurs in turning aside from the primary purpose. I am there primarily to worship God, to seek God, and to be found by God. Whatever the particular vocabulary, religions begin with this end in mind.

Before looking at Christianity's ways of connecting, it will be useful to examine how some other religions go about seeking and moving toward God. Is there a common practice running through the efforts of all worshipers, some discipline that might be seen as essential? We can learn by looking at religions that have lasted and by noticing those practices which satisfy spiritual hunger. We benefit by seeing what "works."

Detachment

A clue that can guide us in spotting the common spiritual practice found in each faith is summed up by psychiatrist Gerald May. "God creates us for love and freedom; attachment hinders us, and grace is necessary for salvation."[4] So what, exactly, is *attachment*? It is that to which we bond, that is, attach. And so, what is *detachment*, as we are using it here? It is not indifference, as we so often think, but the breaking of an overpowering bond.

British theologian Evelyn Underhill described healthy detachment as "love without claimfulness." Each faith tradition recognizes this truism. What "works" is to detach from what is not God and turn our attention wholly toward God. Detachment, in this sense, means not to be controlled by some thing or someone. The first of the Ten Commandments deals head-on with the attachment/detachment issue: God is to come first with us, and we are to worship God only. Anything else is an "idol" and something from which to *detach*. Becoming dependent on that which is other than God is what causes us to lose love and freedom. It is truly said, "We have populated this world with small, mean gods of narrow vision and cold embrace."[5]

In trying to convince her that she should marry him, one of my sons-in-law declared to my daughter that he loved her with all his heart. Knowing her inner conflict about making a lifetime commitment, he assured her that if she refused his offer, he would be deeply saddened, but not destroyed. That is freedom. Had he said, "I cannot live without you," and actually meant that, he would have been making his happiness her responsibility not a thing we should do to anyone. Only detached, nondependent love can love truly. Saying he would not be destroyed by her refusal was the act of one who loves without contaminating self-interest, that is, a true love.

The best story about detachment that I know is one told about Jesus, and it is also the Gospel account that makes us most uncomfortable. We call it the story of "The Rich Young Ruler." If we are honest, we don't like this short scene because it sounds so unfair. A wealthy young man comes to Jesus asking what he should do to "inherit eternal life," which might be like asking for spiritual wholeness. He claims to have followed the commandments faithfully all of his life. Then, and here is the shockingly unfair part, Jesus tells him to sell everything he owns and distribute it to the poor. The Gospel of Luke (18:18-23) tells us that the man, saddened, turns away. And we don't blame him. After all, who in his right mind would give away all his money?

But the encounter is not about money—rather, it is about detachment. If the man had not been so attached to his possessions, to his identity as one who had it all, there would have been no need for Jesus to highlight his addiction by asking him to sell everything. If he had been able to say, "I'd rather keep everything to enjoy, but if I lose it all, I will not be destroyed," then we would know that his possessions gave him pleasure, but that they were not his life's chief concern. In other words, he would have "had no other gods," as the first of the Ten Commandments enjoins. His attachment to God would have been primary. On reading the story, my question to myself is to ask how Jesus would tailor his teaching to me. What idol would he ask me to jettison? No wonder this passage makes us squirm.

It will do us no good to dismiss religions other than our own as irrelevant. Most are growing in numbers and experiencing a renewal in interest and devotion among their members. We need to understand their power, asking ourselves what it is in these traditions that is satisfying to followers. Before asking questions of Christianity, let us make a very brief survey and notice four other traditions, each seeking the God-connection in its own way: Hinduism, Buddhism, Islam, and Judaism.

Hinduism

Hindus seek union using ideas of attachment and detachment. The name they give to the supreme reality they seek is *Brahman*. Hinduism teaches that as long as a person is attached to physical circumstances, he or she is to that degree detached from *Brahman*, a term that represents the concept of absolute reality, utter bliss, pure consciousness, and Being itself. The overattachment we feel toward our own small lives, possessions, and powers prevents us from union, and subjects us to discontent and frustration. The process of detachment from the ego-self, so that one may move toward the infinite, is accomplished through a variety of personal disciplines, making practicing Hindus among the most disciplined devotees among the major religions. There are many other features that characterize Hinduism, some very different from Western practice, but it is useful to notice how self-transcendence and union with the Absolute is approached. Hindu notions of renouncing distracting influences are really not so foreign to us, and remind us of Jesus' admonition that the one who gains his or her life must first lose it. Essentially Jesus was talking about attachment and detachment, concepts central to both Hinduism and Christianity.

Buddhism

Hinduism provided the soil out of which Buddhism grew in that its founder, Siddhartha Gautama, became dissatisfied with the way Hinduism was practiced during his youth. Religious ritual of the time had lost its original purpose and had become mechanical, superstitious, and unavailable to common people. The sense of a felt connection to God had disappeared. Siddhartha felt the deadness of perfunctory practices and determined to find a better path. He searched for a way to escape the sort of sleepwalking he observed in religious formalities and, after years of meditation, found his solution.

What he taught his followers is what we see today as the goal of Buddhist practice, to "wake up." This wakefulness involves looking at life as it truly is, a life that includes suffering as well as joy, and becoming fully aware of all personal experience. Western psychology would call this getting rid of our defenses and denial systems. What interests us here is the method used to approach union with God, in this case, what Buddha called the Unborn. Pain, thought the Buddha (Siddhartha), is caused by personal desire which, when frustrated, causes suffering. In other words, our boundaries are our undoing. The path to bliss is the loosing of these restrictive boundaries and moving toward the boundless self which is called *nirvana*, a state of inner freedom which can no more be captured or quantified than the wind. If one no longer desires that which may disappoint, one is finally free to seek that which does not disappoint—the Ultimate.

Again we see the theme of attachment and detachment. I am reminded of the Gospel story of Jesus and Nicodemus when Jesus compared God's spirit to the boundless wind. Nicodemus was unable to detach from a literal formula for how one approaches God. Jesus' message to him was that connection with God was about relationship and not about rules or techniques. A significant difference in Buddhist and Christian views is that in Buddhism the goal of the quest does not involve a personal deity but a state of being, whereas for Jesus, nothing could have been more intimate than the windlike Spirit, or more personal than "the Father." Although the destination pictured may differ, the path in both Buddhism and Christianity is one that suggests the importance of a growing nondependence on circumstance, other people's opinions, and "things."

Islam

If Buddhism feels somewhat misty and amorphous, Islam, by contrast, is literal and quite definite. Islam, Judaism, and Christianity are all within the Abrahamic family of religions and each worships *the* one God, not *a* god. In Islam, the word *Allah* literally means "the God." Islamic buildings of worship emphasize this monotheism by prohibiting representations of humans or animals in the decor, just as does Judaism. Evidence of this is seen in the wonderfully intricate geometric carvings left by the Moors on walls of the Alhambra in Spain as well as other mosques. The message of this architectural innovation is clear. The worshiper is to think of God, and not of something that stands in for God. We detach from idols by removing their images, shifting our attachment to God.

In the sixth century C.E., Islam found its full development in the teachings of the prophet, Muhammad. He testified that he had received directly from Allah the *Koran*, a book that became the foundation for Islam and remains so today. The Koran is the Muslim's manual for living. It tells how one is to act and to live, making the strict keeping of these precepts the central feature of devotion. Facing Mecca five times a day to kneel and pray keeps the follower constantly aware of God, and it is this repeated practice that constitutes the Muslim's religious formation. The awareness of God engendered by prayers, plus the specific ethical conduct spelled out in the Koran, is what Islam is about. Feelings may come and go, but obedience is the tie to God that binds.

Among Muslim worshipers there is a relatively small group known as the Sufi. Sufis are the "something more" people within Islam, those who seek after a felt experience of God. Their method in seeking God is embodied in the doctrine of *fana,* which means extinction. This is not the extinction of their consciousness but of their *self*-consciousness. The Sufi strives to see the self as a part of God, not separate from God. The "separate self" is the self that lives life pursuing its own agenda, concerned with power, things, and external feedback. Here again we are dealing with concepts of attachment and detachment. Sufis may be heard to say the name of *Allah* again and again, repeating it until the "allness" of God becomes a living realization within their very souls. This repeating of words and phrases is a form of "recollection," and can be found in other religions. One of history's greatest mystical writers is the Sufi poet Rumi, who wrote so accurately about the spiritual journey:

> Whether one moves slowly or with speed,
> the one who is a seeker will be a finder.
> Always seek with your whole self,
> for the search is an excellent guide on the way.[6]

Judaism

Jewish spirituality assumes God's presence in the world. An observant Jew may wonder why God does or does not do something, but never whether God *is*. "At bottom," says one scholar, "Judaism is less a systematic structure of interlocking theological propositions than it is a way of life."[7] This is not an otherworldly spirituality that seeks escape from the endless wheel of life, but a religion that focuses on the tangible now-world and engages its civic problems. Where you find Judaism, you find a concern for law, healing, and social justice. We in the West are so saturated with Judaism's precepts in every area of our lives that we hardly recognize how affected we are by them. A recent and popular book by Thomas Cahill, *The Gifts of the Jews,* attempts to rectify this lack of awareness. "Democracy," says Cahill, "grows directly out of the Israelite vision of *individuals*, subjects of value because they are images of God, each with a unique and personal destiny. There is no way that it could ever have been 'self-evident that all men are created equal' without the intervention of the Jews."[8] The author reminds us that technology, our sense of time as past-present-future, and even observing the "weekend," are also structures given to us by Judaism. This is a highly practical version of attachment and detachment. Torah spirituality implies a daily lived-out allegiance to what God wants for the world rather than a focus on individual self-interest.

The important connection to God is sought in two major ways: prayer and study. Most frequently, prayer is conducted in community, with prayers said both in one's own language and in Hebrew. But it is the reverence for study that has marked Jewish spirituality since 70 C.E. and the destruction of the Jerusalem Temple. To put it in the terms we've been using, reading is recollection. The revered rabbi, Hillel, is noted for declaring to an impatient pagan, "Go forth and learn!"

The Torah, consisting of the first five books of what Christians call the Old Testament, along with other writings about the Torah, is the text which is endlessly examined and interpreted. God's law is preeminent; it is not meant to be mindless rule-keeping, but an interiorized "way of being." From these documents which have been foundational to Western culture, we find Judaism's spirituality, a hands-on involvement that connects to God by means of a good life in the good world that God has made. The deed and the mystery are one.

Christianity

If one wonders how, exactly, Christians seek relationship with God, one must first find out which Christians are being talked about. If they are Roman Catholic or perhaps Anglican, spiritual connection may be most deeply felt in the celebration of the Eucharist. Being part of the Church, the corporate Body of

Christ, could be the important avenue of access for a communicant in the Eastern Orthodox Church. And if the Christian we're discussing is a Protestant, well, which kind? At last count there were at least twenty-seven varieties of Baptists. For some in the Reform tradition, the connection is found chiefly in the study of biblical scripture, reverently referred to as the Word of God; for others, it resides within a felt experience of God's presence at an identifiable conversion moment. There are over nine hundred Christian sects or denominations in the United States alone, so determining a shared spirituality for Christianity is problematic, at best. But there is one thing that unites. The one common denominator among Christians, the centerpiece, so to speak, is the person of Jesus. It is because of him, a Jewish rabbi, that the Christian religion exists.

Following the Recollected Man

One who intends to follow the Christian faith would be wise to look to the person of Jesus for clues as to how to have an intimate and continuous relationship with God. Jesus' identity and his relationship to God are much debated today. Is he the *only* son of God, the second member of the Trinity, or is he the supreme human exemplar whom, because of his life, God honors, or perhaps deifies? Christians, whatever their specific theologies about Jesus, must agree that his mission was to point to "the Father," as he himself described that mission to be. Jesus' continual and constant referral of all to God was his life's theme, rooted in his relationship with God. Theologian Edward Schillebeeckx believes that Jesus' "Abba experience" was basic to his entire life and preaching. The word *Abba* came from Jewish family life of the period and is the familiar term for Father. Its equivalent today would be "papa" or "daddy." Jesus used the term in addressing God when he prayed. "What Jesus had to say about God as man's salvation," says Schillebeeckx, "springs directly from his personal experience of God, of the reality which in his own, for the time extraordinary, way he referred to as *Abba*."[9] This connectedness was distinctive of Jesus' spiritual life. His familiar intimacy with *Abba* was God-consciousness carried to its ultimate degree.

Another distinctive feature rising out of this relationship was that of compassion. Jesus' Sermon on the Mount contains the fundamental statement which informs all other sayings and all his reported activities. He said, "Be merciful, just as your Father is merciful" (Luke 6:26). The Jerusalem Bible translates it "Be you compassionate, as your Creator in Heaven is compassionate." When writing about Jesus, German theologian and martyr Dietrich Bonhoeffer called him "a man for others," a perfect summary description of Jesus' orientation. We see in the Gospel accounts that his feelings of compassion became externally realized in numerous acts of healing. Time and again Jesus finds a suffering person, or they find him, and he acts in their behalf to relieve their distress or lack of wholeness. This is the living out of *tikkun olam*, a Hebrew phrase meaning "to repair the world."

We notice another important feature of Jesus' life-in-God, the value he placed on the interior life. He is constantly asking questions or making statements about our inner being. He illustrated the unexamined life by describing cups that are clean on the outside but dirty inside, and whitewashed graves that contain corruption. He complimented John the Baptist, whom he said was the greatest among men, because of what John was inside himself. When we recall what is known about John the Baptist, we can agree that what he appeared to be on the outside was not his most winning feature. John's life was not lived "on the surface." Like John, Jesus continuously called for self-scrutiny, for conversion, and for a change of heart *(metanoia)* in his hearers and disciples. Surprise, surprise! Jesus asks for detachment from what distracts us. He asks us to make an about-face toward God. It is the interior, spiritual life that leads to the real, authentic self, not the outward trappings. The center of oneself is discovered in the presence of the Creator. We call this process of discovery prayer.

Even with this interior orientation, Jesus was not in the least "otherworldly." He was embedded in the daily rounds of human life, a distinctively Jewish approach to spirituality. He seems not to have bought into the popular Hellenistic dualism about spirit being good and matter being bad. He participated thoroughly in his human life, enjoying friendships, dinner parties, and storytelling. In fact, the contexts and settings for his stories were the familiar events he found around him in nature, in *matter*. He saw his natural life as being permeated by God and not separate from God. God was everywhere: in him, in others, in the world, and over all. To miss that fact was, for Jesus, to miss out on the kingdom of God. And so he would begin his teaching stories with the invitation to "behold," or "look at this!"

There was another outgrowth from Jesus' consciousness of God. When you read through the Gospels, one thing that becomes vividly clear about him is his sense of inclusiveness. To be God-connected in the profound way in which Jesus was will lead us to accept "the other." His caring extended to and included women and men, other racial groups, young and old, wealthy and poor, enemies, and those around him who did not understand him or have a faintest notion about what his life was about. The Gospels show just how far this inclusiveness went by relating Jesus' story of an injured man being rescued by a passing Samaritan, a person whom some of Jesus' hearers rejected as unworthy. In the telling, the Samaritan becomes the hero of the story by taking care of the beaten victim. In conclusion, Jesus admonishes his hearers to be the kind of "neighbor" the Samaritan was (Luke 10:30-37). In another account, Jesus intervenes to prevent the public abuse of a woman caught in adultery. "He who is without sin among you," he said, "let him be the first to throw a stone at her" (John 8:7 NASB). His attachment was to God and God's work in the world, and not focused on the important people he knew and who he was "seen with." He was entirely detached from the lure of fame and reputation.

It is not that whatever people did, good or bad, was of no consequence to him, but that they themselves were acceptable. In his relationship with Mary, the sister of Martha, Jesus demonstrates his belief that women can deal with spiritual and religious truth; this particular woman could and he knew it, because he saw her as a person, not merely a category. He was passionately interested in the rich young ruler, but equally touched by lepers, the sick, and those who were hungry and destitute. He went outside his racial boundaries and even his sense of where his mission lay and became concerned about the life of an outcast woman he met beside a well. It appears that one who becomes deeply connected to *Abba*, will increasingly include "the other."

Detachment requires that something be relinquished, which implies a kind of dying that must take place before a new attachment may be formed. Death appears as a theme prominent in Jesus' own teaching. When he talks about dying, what he usually means is giving up our wish to make ourselves the center of all concern, a theme we have seen in other religious traditions. He also speaks of dying to the "world," that is, the security we posit in the material things we have. The famous story of the rich young ruler is not about the evil of money but is about over-attachment. Had the young man not been so dependent for his security on what he had, Jesus' request that he sell all he owned would have been unnecessary. The request served to reveal to him his enslavement. If he had sold all he possessed, he would then have needed to depend entirely on God. That, the man believed, was too risky, and so he went away, and everyone, including Jesus, was sad. We become uneasy reading the story because it causes the same anxiety in us that it did in the rich young man. Bonhoeffer says, "When Christ calls a man, he bids him come and die."[10] We are too inclined to think of only physical death when we hear this, and it feels far too negative and life-denying for us to consider. But what we are called to do is separate ourselves from the things that do not actually fulfill us, that is, to die to our obsessive need for them. In the life of Jesus, that issue presented an excruciating decision on his part having to do with losing his own physical life; but in this decision, as well as in all decisions made during his adult life, the emphasis had to do with ultimate trust, on where he would place it, or on whom he would place it.

An important question remains. Just how did Jesus go about staying God-connected? First, he seems to have alternated his exposure to people with times of retreat and intentional prayer. And second, he appears to have been praying when he was not in retreat, even in the midst of human contact and interaction. This practice is seen most clearly in his healing encounters. It is as though the first habit, that of retreat, nourished the second, which was the continuous maintaining of a consciousness that God was both in and with him. It is the cultivation of this dual consciousness that we shall be learning about in subsequent chapters.

The times of deliberate retreat, of "getting away," are evident. We first see his need for time alone following his walking away from village life and deciding to begin his prophetic vocation. In order to sort things out and determine exactly those underpinnings on which he would conduct all that he said and did, he needed to be alone and wrestle through his choices. For more than a month he stayed in the desert. Notice that his rejection of organizing his life around comfort, possession, and power over others, was an exercise in total detachment. When he returned from the desert, Luke tells us, "Jesus returned to Galilee in the power of the Spirit" (4:14 *a* NASB). His attachment to God was complete. In his later conversation with the rich young ruler, when saying he must leave behind any false security, Jesus knew exactly what he was asking the man to do: he had done it himself.

Throughout his short adult life Jesus is reported to have gone to what the Gospel writers refer to as "solitary places," especially after periods of intense healing and preaching. As celebrity increased and privacy almost vanished, these times alone became necessary islands for centering himself in God. At life's end, when death threatened, he retreated to his favorite garden outside Jerusalem, again wrestling with what he must do. He addressed God and we can sense that this is a conversation between intimates. His last words, while dying, were an extension of that conversation: "Into your hands I commit my spirit," a quotation lifted from his Psalm-saturated memory.[11]

It is important to say what Jesus was doing in his times of retreat. Certainly they were for rest and relief from public pressure. What they were not were spiritual punctuation marks in an otherwise spiritually unconnected life. Rather, these intentional times of prayerful focus sustained Jesus' return to daily life, making it possible for him to remain *recollected*, to use our word for it. Remember the definition of recollected: *the concentration of the attention on the presence of God.* It is this continuous awareness of and attention to God's presence that is the truly stunning feature of Jesus' life. It is what is meant by what we have been calling "the God-connection."

A Foot on the Path

Huston Smith tells of a tribesman who pointed out that "the circles in spider webs are sticky, whereas its radii are not. This means, he said, that if you wander from side to side in life you get stuck, but if you move toward its center you don't."[12] The recollected life is one in which a person edits and limits those pathways that are detours, those sideways roads that are busy, and possibly pleasant, but lead nowhere. It is the radii, those strands leading toward the center, that are followed. Making this path one's choice requires a special sort of discipline and some single-minded attention. Making the choice also means that you and I need to become creative in the triage of our complicated lives. We need to explore what to add or subtract from the daily routine so that we might become centered in God, which is to say, recollected.

In past centuries one such life pattern came to be called a "Rule of Life." It was lived out in monastic communities and would seem not in any way to fit into our present lives. We have reason to despair of ever having the luxury of what seems to us to be a tranquil and uninterrupted attachment to the Holy. We try to get away for brief periods of time, only to return to things as they were, wondering if we have resources to maintain the spiritually high moments we experienced. Do we have time for such an archaic practice as a daily rule of life? And if we took the time, is it even possible, in this century, to do such a thing? Would it be realistic to suppose one could detach from twenty-first century distractions long enough to become God-focused? If, indeed, it were possible to create a Rule of Life that could be practiced today, what on earth would it look like? We are back where we started, asking "Is that all there is?"

❧ CHAPTER TWO
What Is a Rule?

Our task is the opposite of distraction. Our task is to help people concentrate on the real but often hidden event of God's active presence.
—Henri J. M. Nouwen

A Rule is most often a chosen daily pattern of life and is arranged so that there are particular moments in the day when certain things are done. Sometimes the patterns are arranged around the week, the month, or particular anniversaries in the church year. Most of us unconsciously follow some sort of daily routine, even though we may not think of it as a rule. I know many people for whom a cup of coffee and the morning newspaper are essentials marking the start of the day. Others of us habitually do certain things on certain days. For instance, we may grocery shop, play golf, or go to lessons on the same day of each week. At bedtime we carry out our most elaborate routines. We like the security of feeling that after we have done *this*, followed by *that*, and then one other thing, we are ready to sleep. None of us deliberately lives each day with everything up for grabs, unless, of course, we find ourselves in some emergency situation with our life completely out of control. Typically, we rule ourselves with habits of serial behavior that make our lives flow more easily, and follow sequences that help us to remember what comes next.

A Rule of Life, as the ancients called it, is a pattern of daily actions chosen to accomplish something. The goal of a Rule is *recollection*. With that as a beginning, we can go farther and say that all religious Rules begin as patterns of remembrance, ways of recalling. The Christian tradition of praying at fixed hours is a legacy from Judaism. A prayer called the *Amidah* was said, and in Orthodox practice is still said, three times a day: morning, afternoon, and evening.[1] The goal of a Rule is the continuous remembrance of God. In a later chapter we will explore specific ways to craft a Rule of Life for ourselves, using from the past those things that will help us to creatively adapt what we do to our own century.

Restrictive Rule/Liberating Rule

But first, it may be a good thing to stop and acknowledge that the word "rule" itself has negative associations for many of us. As a progressively individualizing people, a society that values highly the ideas of freedom, especially personal freedom, we resist rules. We want space to express ourselves and to choose what we do based on what we perceive to be our true needs. For us, freedom is having options. Rules, we think, limit this freedom.

We experience the limitations of rules all the time, of course. Someone goes on a shooting rampage, and rules are made restricting gun use. Someone drives too fast, killing a busload of people, and speed limits are set or legal alcohol levels are lowered. A foreign nation goes to war, an expensive military intervention is mounted, and citizen taxes are raised. We sense that we are at all times hemmed in by the effects of actions being taken outside ourselves. And of course, when we break the rules on our own, there are other rules about how society will penalize our conduct. We often fail to notice that some rules provide freedom: restricting gun use may offer freedom from fear for children; limiting blood alcohol may free us, to some degree, from bodily injury caused by highway mayhem; and so forth.

Nevertheless, the word "rule" has a bad reputation with those of us who have been burned by restrictions and the loss of personal options. The Rule about which we speak does not have to do with harmful limitations. Above all, this Rule is about *free-*

dom. Think about it: What restricts our optimal functioning is our very tendency to become distracted by small concerns, to become absorbed in the trivial. A Rule that helps us to stay centered, focused on the Creator of life, brings perspective and clarity to that life. How freeing it would be if we felt ourselves at all times to be in God's presence, and what a difference such a sense of that accompanying Presence would make.

When we look at those people who make a difference, both in history and today, one common characteristic seems to be their ability to *triage time*. To triage suggests the ability to sort out and to let go of some good things in order to choose the best. The *Oxford American Dictionary* describes triage as "a sorting according to quality,"[2] a definition that extends past the word's use in medical circles. People who make a mark decide what is most important in their lives and eliminate anything that does not directly contribute to their chosen goal. They are people who, knowingly or unknowingly, craft a Rule of Life for themselves.

An example is Benjamin Franklin, one of the more productive figures in American history. In his autobiography he says that at one time he constructed for himself what he calls a "liturgy," or form of prayer, for his daily private use. In addition, Franklin listed all the virtues he wished for himself: temperance, silence, order, frugality, industry; in all, a total of thirteen. He set about to keep these by making a little book in which, he says, "I allotted a Page for each of the Virtues."[3] A grid was drawn on each page so that the week's progress could be recorded. As to his daily rule, he chose to ask himself one question each morning: "What Good shall I do this day?" Again in the evening, he called himself to account with the question, "What Good have I done today?"[4] Franklin is candid in telling the reader that his original list contained only twelve virtues to which he later added a thirteenth. This was due to the comment of a Quaker friend who accused him of being entirely too proud of always being right, and resulted in Franklin adding to his list the virtue of "humility."

We could spend pages upon pages citing the names of effective people who illustrate the power of a deliberately focused life. Stephen Covey, in his popular book *The 7 Habits of Highly*

Effective People, explains how first choosing and then acting is essential to the satisfying life.[5] We may not be as obsessive as Franklin, making a written record of each day's progress, but if the goal of our life is companionship with God, we will need to first construct, then carry out, a Rule of Life aimed to accomplish that end.

A Short History of the Rule

The sort of Rule being described here as a continual remembrance of God began, so far as we know, in the early part of the fourth century. There were men, and later women, who chose to leave what they experienced as a corrupt society and seek spirituality in the Egyptian desert. Some said they went to "do battle with the devil." I would suspect that what they wanted was to divorce themselves from those things to which they were overly attached. We have referred already to the Gospel story of Jesus' encounter with the rich young ruler, and it was the reading of this very account that prompted St. Antony to sell what he had and seek God in solitude, thereby becoming the first of those whom we now call the Desert Fathers. Some of those who sought a reclusive life later formed communities, and such groupings made it expedient for them to form a Rule, which is to say, a pattern of daily living that would carry out the original intention of those who came to the desert for prayer and spiritual insight.

Pachomius (c. 290–346) began the first of these monastic communities in which daily life was organized around a Rule consisting of work, study of Scripture, and prayer. Later Jerome, biblical translator and the most learned of all the scholars in the early church, adapted Pachomius's Rule and established monastic communities of his own. In a society where official religion had become corrupt, these societies of seekers spread, and by the Middle Ages "the proliferation of organizations for maintaining various forms of religious life was a feature of [the] period."[6] Thousands of communities were established, each with distinctive Rules, and by the end of the thirteenth century six or eight major types of community had evolved with close to twenty derivative branches.

Why?

Why is it important to know about early monastic Orders if you and I do not plan to join one? We are not likely to drop out and go to live in the Egyptian desert! Why look into ancient life patterns to which we cannot, indeed may not even want to, adapt ourselves? We may even feel sorry for people who so limited their lives. They chose not to marry and not to own anything (though the Orders to which they belonged often owned much), and they committed themselves with permanent promises, or vows. This is not a lifestyle readily appealing to twenty-first century people, to be sure, and it certainly does not sound like freedom. Further, these early Orders were founded, not only to seek God, but to protect their members from the world. They were islands of safety for some who, for various reasons, could not prosper on "the outside." This sounds to us like an unhealthy way to live, and so the thought of monastic life under a Rule may strike us as unpleasant, even repelling.

Like all human institutions, there is the good and the bad, the light and the dark side. Certainly, these communities should not be idealized by us as perfect societies. Almost all of them began with high intention; some ended in decline, others in total ruin, and still others have survived to this day, but there is a good reason to examine them. Despite their frailties and faults, they did attempt to regulate their lives in such a way as to become spiritually alive, conscious of God's presence at all times, and, ultimately, one with God. It was done chiefly by employing a Rule of Life, a pattern fostering such spiritual depth in some of them that much of Christendom's greatest writing came, and continues to come, from these seekers. The numerous examples overcome our ability to recall: Gregory the Great, Thomas Aquinas, Meister Eckhart, Mechthild of Magdeburg, Bernard of Clairvaux, the Victorines, Catherine of Siena, Hildegard of

Bingen, St. Francis of Assisi, St. John of the Cross, Teresa of Avila, Thomas Merton, and countless others, all living a Rule of Life.

It will not be surprising if some of the writers named above, perhaps all of them, are unfamiliar. We no longer know about them. It is my view that much of the spiritual practice of today tries to reinvent the wheel. Were we to know these writers, and glean from them the fruits of their focused years spent with God, we would not be so much in the dark about what to do with our own spiritual yearnings. That, however, is a subject for another time. What we can do right now is to see how it is that a spiritual discipline developed by these pioneers can enhance our own quest. These were people who approached life with the intention of knowing God, and so ordered their days to that end. They made the effort to triage time.

Life in the Communities

I think we are agreed that entering a modern monastic community is not an option for most of us. People still do it, of course, and there are some strong and effective monasteries and convents, both Roman Catholic and a few Protestant, populated by those who feel a clear call to a separated life. For most of us, however, it will be important to look at the way monastics lived their lives, learning from them the basic principles of a life ordered toward the enjoyment of God. There is no formula here for the recollected life, just suggestions which may prompt other thoughts and creativity on the part of the reader. Each life is different and what is suggested here may not fit everyone. That is where creativity begins. If you believe that a life of continuous companionship with God is possible, then you can look at models of recollection taken from the past and custom design a Rule to fit your present life.

The most pervasive among these communities were those within the Benedictine Order. Its Rule of Life is still maintained today among Benedictine houses as well as some other orders which adopted the Benedictine Rule. It will serve our purpose if we look at this Order and ask ourselves why and how it succeeded, and what caused some of its failures. When reading the Rule of St. Benedict, one is amazed to see how short it is, only a booklet, and how simply the instructions are presented.[7]

Benedict of Nursia was born in 480 into a culture that was disintegrating before his eyes. Rome had twice been sacked and the last emperor was about to be deposed. The social and economic order was collapsing and the Church was being torn to pieces with doctrinal disputes. Young Benedict walked out on city life and its ecclesiastical mess and headed for the countryside, where he might live a simple life dedicated to God. Others, also looking for such a life, clustered around him, and he found himself the leader of a monastic community dedicated to simplicity and prayer. They wanted a Rule of Life to guide them, one that expressed what Benedict himself sought: hospitality, reasonableness, quiet, stability, and above all, prayer. Benedict, drawing from other Rules, tried to put into words the way of life he envisioned for himself and for his new followers. The result is what is called the *via media*, the middle way, which took the best wisdom from many sources and wove them into a balanced life pattern. Scholars see this Rule as a creativity of synthesis. "[Benedict] holds together the emphasis on the solitary, on the withdrawal and disengagement that Cassian taught, with the emphasis from Basil on the communal or shared life. Here are the desert and the city juxtaposed."[8] By the eighth century, Benedict's Rule had spread throughout the Western world and had become a model for other community rules. One of the reasons Benedictine life has lasted until today is simply that the Rule works. It is not about a set of "have-to" prescriptions which restrict, but more about a way of life and an attitude of mind which liberate one to be free to love God.

Daily life in a Benedictine community was, and is today, punctuated by particular times of prayer and study known as Vigils, Lauds, Prime, Terce, Sext, None, Vespers, and Compline. Called "The Hours," these pauses in the normal day occurred at regular intervals beginning at 2:00 A.M. followed by dawn, 6:00 A.M., 9:00 A.M, and then noon. They continued through the afternoon and evening at three, dusk, and bedtime.[9] We flinch when we think about beginning prayer at the early hour of two in the morning, however, we must remember that this society was agricultural and regulated its day by sunlight. These people went to bed early! The thing to notice is not the names of the hours, the times at which they occurred, or even how many times prayers were offered, but that the monks built into their daily life these habitual moments of recollection. We shall explore in chapter 4 how "the hours" can be adapted to our own lives, unlikely as that might seem on first examination.

The important thing we learn from the Benedictines and other Orders is that a person's day actually can be lived out in a *rhythm of remembrance*. Benedict, in fact, patterned his "hours" after those followed by the Roman changing of the guard. We may want to choose some way of punctuating our day that better reflects our own times and contemporary schedules. "I know only too well from my own experience," says historian Esther de Waal, "that a life without boundaries can never become a life that is constructive, creative, or life-giving."[10] The Hours, as they were called, are the boundaries. They provide scaffolding or a framework that supports our connection to God while at the same time allowing for the random and unexpected events that make up each of the twenty-four hours. If one "misses" an hour, then that person just knows that there is another one coming 'round at a later time. What if you were to choose three "hours" as your own: dawn, noon, and evening? Would that be doable? Probably. In fact you may do that already.

A second emphasis in Benedictine life was what he called *stability*. Benedict placed high value on sticking with the place and the task. During this period in society there were some orders know as *mendicant*, those in which monks, in order to carry out their vow of poverty, begged food and substance from the local townspeople. This mobility also made them able to travel in pursuit of their missionary activities. In contrast, Benedict instructed his monks to maintain their own community house, grow their own food, and generally support their lives apart from external obligations. They shared the fruits of their labors with the less fortunate, and generosity and hospitality were encouraged. They were even encouraged to use leisure well, something we will discuss further in a later chapter. The important thing about Benedictine stability was its emphasis on fostering holiness in common daily life rather than on random and occasional spiritual nourishment.

Benedictine life has flourished, waned, and revived—but lasted—for over fifteen hundred years. This way of life focuses on finding the holy within the daily. It honors the regularity of waking and sleeping, of working and leisure, and of a responsible and simple lifestyle. It is not dramatic, at least not circumstantially, and high moments of holy companionship are found as one's ordinary life is lived out in the Creator's extraordinary creation. Joan Chittister, prioress of a Benedictine convent, says that it is not the special places and rarefied conditions that, in the long run, mature one's faith, but rather "daily life is the stuff of which high sanctity can be made."[11] Benedictine spirituality was and is designed for the common person and the average day.

Across centuries, Benedictine houses became the recipients of both property and social position. In time, the preoccupation with asset management and propriety overtook the simplicity of an unencumbered life. And Benedictine lives became distracted (attached) very much like our own. By the eleventh century their spiritual power was largely depleted and new religious orders emerged to fill the void. Two that had success were the Augustine canons and the Cistercian monks. Each was quite different from the other and, interestingly, exemplified different aspects of the original Benedictine virtues. Much of the original intent of Benedict's Rule was recovered and today Benedictine houses continue and flourish. Many have read something about this life in the popular book by Kathleen Norris, *The Cloister Walk*. I recommend it for anyone who would enjoy getting the flavor of contemporary monastic living.[12]

Things to Notice

During the Middle Ages, monastic Orders were the logical destination for those with religious fervor. Although some still take this path today, it is not the choice made by most of us. It will greatly inform us, however, if we can identify useful patterns of behavior within these intentional communities.

The first thing to notice is that when any society becomes chaotic and stressed, people seek alternative ways of living. Those who seek some interior peace and centeredness are especially driven to create another way to live. During the last twenty years, numerous books have been written about and by people in high stress urban lives who forfeit large incomes in order to carve out for themselves simpler and more basic styles of living. Whether you and I choose the more radical "leave it all behind" solution or not, we do yearn for order and some tranquility. And if we are honest, most of us will say we are seeking a spiritual dimension we suspect is there for us.

A second thing to notice in the histories of all religious orders is that they flourish only so long as they are able to stay close to their original intention, to seek and maintain a God-focused life. It is when their lives, corporate and personal, became overwhelmed with external detail, with maintenance of a life that no longer made sense, that things went bad. Is it any different for us? Did you enter law or medicine or business with an original intention for good? And did you become swamped with things that have almost nothing to do with your original ideal? We could say this about almost any enterprise for which we had high hopes, including family life. We laugh and write off our disillusionment as "growing up," but it doesn't feel to us like growth of any kind. It can feel more like death by gradual stagnation. We fantasize changing jobs as a solution. Those seeking communion with God sometimes imagine that the next religious retreat will do it, especially if the speaker is good and the music moving. Perhaps changing jobs is a good idea, and certainly a religious retreat can be energizing, but the Rule points us to *redeeming the daily* rather than escaping it. The retreat and the workshop can give that crucial shove in the right direction, but the Rule says that it is in life's "givens" that we find the holy.

The quintessential expression of this attitude is found in the life and writing of the seventeenth-century Carmelite monk

Brother Lawrence. It was said that "with him the set times of prayer were not different from other times," and that "his greatest business did not divert him from God."[13] God, for Brother Lawrence, is in everything and over everything. God is already here and is not found by going elsewhere. Our task is to convert our minds toward seeing this truth, toward seeing that all is holy and that the Holy One is in all we see. Otherwise, we will find ourselves chasing greener pastures for the rest of our exhausted lives.

Reasons for a Rule

Most of us have been on diets and exercise plans designed to help us lose weight or to reform our bodies in some way we think is desirable. The shame experienced when we go off the wagon, so to speak, is a commonplace. We discover one day that we are no longer doing what we set out to do, and that it is all much too difficult. Will it be the same with a resolve to lead our lives in a patterned way, to lead a life recollected to God? It could, especially if we become rigid and obsessive in carrying out what we interpret to be "demands." It will fail if we think of it as a technique that will get us something, such as moral goodness or lowered blood pressure. It will succeed if we gradually and naturally learn to incorporate reminders of God's presence into the life we already live.

The reason a Rule works is that it is based not only on devotion, but on association. I can smell a particular kind of cigar smoke and immediately envision Christmas at my maternal grandmother's house. This memory is powerful for me, and inevitable, because my uncle, who was always there, smoked a cigar throughout the celebration and did so each Christmas that I can remember. Some of you, to this day, cannot eat a certain food because you associate it with becoming sick years ago. Is there a place which, when you go there, brings you joy and a sense of peace? Why does that particular place give you peace more that other places?

For each of us, certain circumstances always evoke religious feelings. Some people, many who are older, cannot sit down to a dinner table without feeling the impulse to bow their heads. Those who grew up in the earlier part of this century may have come from families where they always said "the blessing." This prayer was said in my own childhood home, and I recall going to a little friend's home and thinking their food would be poisoned because the blessing had not been said over it. An association that strong lasts.

Liturgy, the patterns we make for our gathered worship, helps us largely because of what we associate with the gestures and sounds over time. It is because these associations are so important to us that we create ritual. In his most recent book, liturgist William Seth Adams begins by saying, "The human spirit requires ritual. The stories we tell, the myths that shape us and give us meaning, need to be acted out."[14] We learn through our pores, someone has said, meaning that we internalize the environment, especially if it is a repeated experience in our lives. We worry about children watching violence on television for exactly this reason.

I recall being somewhat distressed at having "drifted off" during a worship service, to which the minister responded, "Don't worry about it. The liturgy is there to pick you up again." And it does. The liturgical framework both liberates and holds. I was being allowed to "come back," and when I regained focus, the Christian story was continuing to be acted out, as it has been each Sunday morning, and will be again next Sunday. I could again enter worship. The Rule, as we shall see, creates a structure (a liturgy) of "hours," nodal points in every day which recall God's presence by associating that presence with common, daily things. The common things are the very reminders that gather our thoughts, pulling us back to center. What could be more common than bread or water or wine? During the liturgy we may allow these ordinary elements to recall deeply felt moments of God-with-us. And each time we use them, we expose ourselves to the possibility of again being transformed.

Repetition and association are key to a sustained spiritual life. Intermittent inspirational moments have their important place and are the initial reason most of us seek the "something more." But finally, it is in the daily common life that we find our deepest growth. There are those who have gone before us who also believed in the value of regularity of sustained religious life. They worked out daily patterns of prayer that may be useful to us in our own time if we but learn how to adapt to our own century the legacy of their insights.

CHAPTER THREE
The Sacramental Day

Glorify the Lord, O nights and days,
O shining light and enfolding dark.
— "A Song of Creation," Canticle 12, v. 9
The Episcopal Hymnal 1982, S-229

So far we have determined that we are very busy people, per-haps even frantic ones, and that there must be "something more" than just this perpetual activity. In previous chapters we scanned the major religions and noticed that they, too, wanted something more, and sought it through detachment and recol-lection. Our study has also shown that one of the ways an ear-lier Christian tradition attempted to solve the problem of recollection was to develop a monastic system of living in enclosed community, with different hours of the day marked out for the intentional remembrance of God.

Because of our twenty-first-century lifestyles, the problem of remaining recollected is not now so easily solved. It becomes clear that we need more help. Our problem can be defined as follows:

(1) In order to function in present-day society, we must focus attention not only on work, families, and houses, but on rapid transportation and multiple communication devices, as well as extremely high levels of outside information and stimulation. We often feel overwhelmed.

(2) In past centuries we lived by the sun, but today we live by the clock. We depend on each other to show up on time and pro-duce work by a deadline.

(3) Since mental attention to our environment is stretched, even stressed, we see that the use of energy and time in this century cannot be structured in ways which worked well in the past. Those seeking a God-conscious life are faced with the task of creating new structures, by adapting what was learned in the past to what will work in the present.

The solution is to decide what we want and then restructure the energy and time available to accomplish our goal. But, that sounds impossible, given what we know about our lives as of this moment. If we do not have time for interior nourishment and connection, we just may need to make it possible. Anthony de Mello encourages us by pointing out that "faith comes as a gift from just exposing yourself to God's company."[1] So how might we arrange the exposure?

The Daily as Sacramental

St. Augustine defined a sacrament as the "visible form of invisible grace."[2] What we need is an infusion of this invisible grace about which Augustine writes. Grace might be defined as that breakthrough of God that brings us the very interior nourishment and connection we seek. In our culture of instant gratification, we hope that spiritual life will come easily and quickly, that we will somehow be very quietly invaded by God. A shortcut would be nice, some sort of spiritual event during which our loneliness is overcome and our intentions made pure. We only have to look at what the Church calls the "Sacraments" to see that it is we, ourselves, who must participate in this receiving of grace.

Historically, the Christian church recognized seven sacraments: baptism, confirmation, the Eucharist, penance, extreme unction, orders, and matrimony. Baptism and Eucharist (communion) became the two observances of Protestantism. The truth is that *everything* is, or can be, a sacrament, depending on how we see things. The sacraments of the Church mark milestone moments in our human passage, asking us to stop and accept the awesome presence of God in such moments. In

Christian life, baptism and Communion are paramount because they were exemplified by Jesus. We should not miss, however, the sacramentality of all moments. Rabbi Menchen Mendal has said, "Whoever does not see God in every place does not see God in any place."[3] How might we accustom ourselves to see God in every place? How can each day be sacrament, an experience of God-with-us?

All Is Holy

Our starting place, the foundation on which we must build, is the central tenet of Benedictine life, the belief that all is holy. If we agree to this life view as our basic premise, then our schemes for working out a recollected life in our time must grow out of that belief. For many years those of us in the West have divided experience into the "real" and the other kind. We have efficiently separated the exterior, palpable world, the kind that can be named, categorized, and measured, and called it real. What was left was our interior life, that inner activity of self-reflection and transcendence. We love categories and have divided things into two very distinct parts, the secular and the sacred. Now we suspect that we may have gone too far with this divorce of realities. We are beginning to understand that human beings may rely on *both* realities, not just one or the other. People are made by the Creator to know both realities, and so, are creatures-of-a-piece. The transcendent is as real as the palpable, the inner experience as real as the outer experience. In a word, we are beginning to trust our inner perceptions.

The biblical text agrees with this recently returning notion. The first chapter of Genesis declares that "God saw *all* that [God] had made, and indeed, it was very good" (Genesis 1:31 NASB, italics mine). All we see and sense, exterior and interior, is equally real, was made good by God, and is therefore a clue about God. And, by the way, the visible and touchable world is no less a revelation of God than is the transcendent. Balance of perception between the visible and the invisible yields the truest conclusion. It is much like seeing with two eyes rather than one.

Each eye sees the same thing but from a slightly different vantage point, thus giving us a more accurate picture.

Substitutes for Spirituality

If we take as a given the belief that all is holy, we may then set out to craft a way of noticing that the holy is all around us. I want to suggest a way to do that, one that borrows from the successes of past practice and hopes to adapt to the present life realities. But we must be careful in how we work out methods of remembrance. Social researcher, Robert Wuthnow commenting on current religious life, offers a warning to those constructing new ways to have more spiritual lives. "The point of spiritual discipline is not to encase the soul in rigid rules but to give it room to maneuver and to grow. . . . The sacred is always too powerful to be tamed by simple formulas and techniques."[4] We do not need a new, obsessive slavery to a hierarchy of rules. Trudging mindlessly through motions and prayers is not a substitute for deeply experienced worship. One thing the past has taught us is that when a discipline loses the heartfelt spirit that gave rise to it in the first place, that discipline becomes a tyranny. When "I yearn" becomes "I have to," something dies. The monastics, who first observed a Rule of Life, would have defeated their holy purpose if, in the course of long years or by their inattention, they had seen their daily discipline as nothing more than a chore to be gotten through. Unthinking doggedness is not the approach to spiritual discipline that we need. On the other hand, Wuthnow offers the important caveat that spirituality also "requires practice, a serious engagement with the sacred that moves one beyond the realities of everyday life."[5]

This second admonition by Wuthnow is as important as the first. Unless we are intentional and deliberate, unless we give some thought and energy to how we will foster a deeper awareness of God, we will always wish for it, but never have it. It will not be ours because of our longing alone. We may listen to scores of charismatic speakers, frame inspirational quotations, buy spiritual music on CDs and figurines of angels, engage in scraps of ritual borrowed from many traditions, and generally do anything to "feel religious," but without a steady, long-term way to live our common days in God's presence, our sense of that Presence will be fleeting. As one journalist put it, "In best-seller heaven, there are angels (hark, a whole host of them) jamming the roads less traveled with soul mates embracing the light in their search for the celestine prophecy."[6] The author is making a point through ridicule, and the quotation does not include the legitimate contribution to increased spiritual life of some of these influences. Her point, however, is legitimate. *We bootleg our spiritual experience from sources other than from our direct experience of God.* We seek a religion exported to us by writers, magical objects and places, compelling speakers, heightened group experiences, televangelists, or celestial beings. Some reader may even be seeking it from this book. It is not that these things are bad; they simply are *not* the "primary text."

A primary text, scholars will tell you, is the original writing, not a commentary on that writing. When we were in school, most of us preferred to buy books by authors who read the primary text for us, and then, in more easily understood language, explained what the original author was saying. We got second-hand what we might have had firsthand, had we had the courage to engage the original writer. Let's make this simple: *God is* the primary text. A direct experience of God and a sustained daily friendship with the Creator is the source, the very fountainhead, of spiritual life. Other things will help, indeed may point the way to this constant connectedness, but they are no substitute for it. There is no substitute for God.

Those who rely on secondary texts plead that they do so because there is not enough time to wade through the original, or that they want someone else to do the work by condensing it, or even that the original is just "too hard." In the case of text-books, some of these complaints may wash, but the objections do not apply to our relationship with God. First, we have time for those enterprises and relationships about which we most deeply care. Second, we may benefit from reading or knowing about those who have, so to speak, done the hard work; but their experience cannot stand in for our own. The last objection by the would-be scholar is that the original is too difficult to understand. For beginning academics, this is often the case and an easier and more accessible version of the original ideas may be the best path. But God, unlike books, adapts to us. God comes to us as we are, speaks in our language, and honors our limitations. We are absolutely wrong when we imagine that God is "too hard." We must come to terms with the fact that God is simply not found in the Cliff Notes.

Praying the Hours: A Way of Awareness

We will begin with what we know has proved useful to those who have gone before in this quest. And let us agree that we will discard what does not fit our needs. I propose that we use as our model "The Hours," those daily pauses that punctuated the monastic day. Our goal will be to create for ourselves a continuous and easy familiarity with the fact of God's presence in each day. Some will choose to begin with the observance of only two or three of the hours, not all eight, which may seem impractical, if not daunting. Whatever we choose, we are looking for a rhythm of remembrance that works for us.

Keep in mind that we are not talking about sixty-minute hours, but about times of pausing in the day, however brief or long. "The Psalmist's cry 'Seven times a day do I praise thee because of thy righteous judgments' (Psalm 119:164) anticipated, centuries before Christ, what was to become the Church's practice."[7] The psalmist's words were written at a time when clocks as we know them were not in use. It's interesting that these hours were, and still are, called *canonical* hours. *Canon* is the name for a unit of measure or a standard of some sort, which explains why we speak of the canon of scripture, that is, the standard collection. But the word canon also means a trellis of the kind that supports vines, and thinking of the hours in this way helps us in what we are about to do. Interpreted as a structure, the canonical hours become the support system, the outline, the grid, or the trellis, so to speak, of our daily spiritual practice. (The same can be said for the cycle of the church year, which many churches observe: spring brings the celebration of Easter; the winter, Advent and Christmas; and then Lent leads again to Easter. This framework is experienced as a progression in the life of Jesus.)

The monks called their carrying out of all these hourly observances the *Opus Dei*, the work of God. Today we describe them as leading what we call "a contemplative life." But anyone, then or now, who leads a life of regularly observing thoughtful moments of remembrance, may be said to be a contemplative. The question we want to address is how we will carry out the *Opus Dei* in our own lives. The monastic pattern for the hours was to meet together as a community at each of the assigned hours, read or sing the scriptures, and pray out loud in unison. Typically, this is not possible for us during our workday, but let us see if some translation into twenty-first century life can be made. Let us try to understand the principles that underlie "the hours," and interpret those understandings into what we do during our own day. Gabriel O'Donnell says that the "Prayer of the Hours consecrates time, not by changing it and making it other than it is, but by admitting it to be *what it is already*—God's time."[8]

Vigils

This hour is sometimes called Matins, and is often combined with the next hour, Lauds. One can see why it is given little attention, even eliminated from the rotation. How would you like to get up at three or four in the morning to pray? Of course, if you went to bed at seven or eight the evening before, as did the monks, you might be more likely not to mind. Bedtime was at sundown for those whose lives were not regulated by the alarm clock. Most of us will wisely choose to skip this hour, but, for some, there is a distinct twenty-first-century use for it. In contemporary life, where we do live by the clock, there is such a thing as the night shift. Like monks, truck drivers and shift workers are also up at wee hours, doing their jobs around the clock. Others watch by a bedside through the night, or are awake with their own worries.

Vigils has another use. Have you ever gone to bed tired, only to awake at three in the morning, your head crowded with anxious anticipation or sad regrets? In a crowded life there is little time in the day to process what we experience, to ponder it awhile and to make sense of life's impact on us. We want to fall asleep but we can't. Unresolved stress wakes us up and invites us to take time for ourselves. Instead of fretting, choose to make this an hour of Vigils, that is, a time to quiet yourself, turning over to God those things you cannot control. Rather than toss about in your bed, get up, refresh yourself, then ask God to stand vigil, that is, to oversee what you cannot. Sit quietly, breathe deeply, relax your body, and give your cares away for a while. They will be safe in God's hands until you can take them up again. The hour of Vigils, for many of us, has a useful place.

Darkness is the nature of Vigils. The darkness holds us in its embrace and conceals all that would distract our thoughts. During the day we suffer overstimulation, scattered intentions, and serial crises. In the deepest part of night, the blackness brings peacefulness and an invitation to go inward. One can hear the distant train whistle, an airplane passing above, and the quiet sound of wind. On the night shift or in the hospital room, there is an intimacy among those who know that few people are up at this hour. The darkness underlines the light. Without it we would not value light nearly so much. When we experience hope, we speak of "a light at the end of the tunnel." The tunnel is a metaphor for the dark passage and the fact that there is light which will finally come.

So how does one pray during Vigils? A Dominican nun has said that the night prayers of the sisters "cleanse the air of the world." Simply experiencing the dark and having thoughts about its meaning *is* prayer. Letting God use the silence to be with us is a kind of union. This is not the time for great effort or grand and complicated prayers. It is a time of companionship and invitation. Just being in the dark and wondering what the still hours have to say is enough. In the Hebrew scripture, Jacob wakes up in the dark. He wrestles with God's angel and says, "I will not let you go unless you bless me." And the angel does!

Lauds

"*Laudate*," sings the choir; the Latin word means "Praise to you." This is one of the hours that has lasted in importance, one that is what we might call an anchor hour within the monastic structure of remembrance. Often the first "office" of the day, it welcomes the light with a hymn, psalms, prayers, and, very appropriate to a good beginning, the Lord's Prayer. We say with the psalmist, "My soul waits for God more than those who watch for the morning" (130:6). Lauds, or praise, is an hour to enjoy! It is the time to pay attention, to be grateful that you at least woke up! We do not know what the day will bring, but for now, for this moment, all is dawning. All is possibility.

So, for what should we pray? One can read a favorite prayer, or pray conversationally about what comes to mind as an immediate concern. A kind of praying that is especially helpful at this hour is to simply sit in quietness with God: no words, few thoughts, quiet breathing. Just "be with." The psalmist declares, "For God alone my soul in silence waits" (62:5 *The Book of Common Prayer*, p. 669). There are scores of people of all religious persuasions, and some with no religion, who depend on this quiet kind of meditation for their day's beginning. It modulates the stress that often begins in us as we hurry to leave the house. There are as many ways to "do" Lauds, as there are people. Reading scripture is good, and so is doing what some groups call "The Daily Office" and others call their "daily devotions."

Of course, you can't get up thirty minutes late and expect to be calm about spending this restful sort of time with God. This is when we have to make a decision about what we really want. If you read this chapter, are inspired, and do nothing to carry it out, you're reading the secondary text. And something else: whatever time you choose to take, don't allow what you do to become mechanical. We do not get God-points for mindlessness.

It is an offense. How would you like a love letter read to you by an impersonal computer voice?

Now the question arises as to how long this "hour" should be. As we've already said, the traditional use of the word referred more to a time of day than to a sixty minute duration. Your "hour" is as long as you need it to be. There will be mornings, for instance Saturdays, when you have plenty of time, perhaps the full sixty minutes that we now associate with an hour. Many times there will be less than ten minutes to pause. But it is always important, especially with Lauds, to wake, to experience gratitude, and to center into a moment of interior quiet and ease with God. Many who are experienced in this morning prayer, say that twenty minutes feels both adequate and manageable.

As you pray, you may think of those you love and of their safety. A prayer for guidance may be needed, especially if you know that you will be meeting a potential crisis. Rather than praying for a particular outcome, ask that you will stay centered in the kind of quiet and confidence you experience at the moment you are praying. During the day you can carry with you the prophet Isaiah's phrase, "In quietness and confidence shall be your strength" (30:15 KJV). The psalmist's words also make a good start if there is likely to be trouble ahead: "Give ear to my words, O LORD. Consider my groaning. Heed the sound of my cry for help, my King and my God, for to Thee do I pray. In the morning, O LORD, Thou wilt hear my voice" (5:1-3 NASB). All the psalms make for good praying.

Lauds announces that the first rays of light are now approaching. Even though you are hurried, don't miss out on the celebration.

Prime

Some modern observances omit this hour, but you will cheat yourself if you do so. Associate this hour with the moment when you check your calender, planner, or the day's agenda, to see what is ahead of you. Here is the day in outline, right in front of you. Only take a minute, no more. Silently acknowledge the presence of God in all your plans. What is before you is your work, and work is holy when done well and for the benefit of all. Decisions will be made. There may be meetings and personal encounters with associates, committee members, and friends. God wants to bless your work and bless you as you do it. Each encounter can be holy if you are conscious of God-in-you at the time. That is what Prime can be about in the twenty-first century. It may be one of the most valuable fragments of time we spend and, though it lasts but a moment, an essential "hour."

Terce

It is now midmorning. The day is underway and it is time for a coffee break, a cup of tea, a glass of water, or a snack. Secretaries take this break more than bosses or homemakers. But everyone feels the need for pause, especially if the work day is several hours old. This is the moment to de-escalate. Calm yourself as much as possible, breathe more slowly, and relax your shoulders. Sip your coffee or go to the watercooler. Look out the window, if there is one, and, as they say, chill out. That's all. You are aware of God being with you because you thought about that during Lauds and Prime. Terce is the "third hour," the morning time when the monks paused for prayer. You may do that, even with your eyes open and as you walk down the hallway. Dr. Pepper advertisements used to show a clock on which were written the words, "The pause that refreshes." That is what Terce is. Deeply breathe in God's spirit and return to the task, refocused and refreshed.

Sext

It is now noon and the day is half done, half waiting. I attended a college that played the Westminster chimes from its tower located in the center of the campus. Those chimes rang every fifteen minutes, each interval with its distinctive tonal pattern. The longest chime, and, it seemed to me, the loudest, was the one at noonday. Almost all of us who were students counted all twelve strokes as they rang out across the tops of buildings. It was when we heard the noonday chime that we became aware that our class should be ending, that we were hungry, and that if we didn't get going, someone would beat us in line. At more thoughtful times, we mentally intoned the words that go with the Westminster chime:

> Lord, through this hour, be thou my guide,
> So by thy power, no foot shall slide.

Some of you, especially those who are older and grew up in a rural setting, may recall a picture, on the wall of a schoolroom or someone's home, called *The Angelus*. In it two middle-aged farm-workers, a man and a woman, have put aside their hoes and are shown with clasped hands and bowed heads. Looking at the soundless print on the wall, one can somehow hear the noonday bells tolling out the hour so that the community can pause to pray. Over time, it became the custom to pray for peace when the Angelus bell sounded,[9] and it is not difficult, especially at noontime, for us to imagine the sun shining over all the world and on those problems we heard about last night on the evening news.

In doing the hours as moments of prayer, we will want, indeed we must, include more than our own concerns. It is likely that you may have in your mind the events reported on a morning television show or seen in an article in your newspaper. And who is to pray for these situations and dilemmas if not we, ourselves? We imagine they are puny prayers and do no good, but we have no evidence of that. Just because what we specifically request does not exactly happen does not mean that the prayer, in God's economy, was not of powerful use. Often, if we do not see a perfect result, we suppose there was no good done at all. We are called upon to be caring and faithful, not to monitor results. Praying for the world is an exercise of faith in a God who says that nothing good is wasted. One cannot even conceptualize the power of focused prayers, offered each day, and said with compassion.

This hour may be as brief as Prime and Terce, which precede it. It all depends on the amount of time available to you. What if you have a luncheon appointment with a friend and no lengthy pause is possible? As food is served, you can silently thank God and remember the world. It will not be much of a stretch, as you look at your plate, to realize that you have food before you and many in the world are in need. It is much more important to make this small remembrance than to despair, thinking that there is no way you can help, and no way you can "do the hours."

There are so many things that can happen because you stop for these moments of recollection. First, you are called into a consciousness of God just as you are about to encounter others. Because of this consciousness, you are more likely to stay centered in that "quietness and confidence" of which Isaiah wrote. Second, your thoughts will be focused on the needs of others, and that compassionate energy is made available to God in order to affect healing and help. And last, because of repeated thoughts of compassion toward the world, you will be more open to those opportunities that enable you to actively contribute to the solutions of problems. No, this small moment is not a waste of time, or an unimportant "hour."

David Steindl-Rast says that the noonday hour is also a time of transition, passing into the second part of the day. "The hour is rousing us to summon the courage to stay the course, to remain true to our ideals through the rest of the day." Prayer, he says, is "attuning yourself to the life of the world."[10] At noon, the world is truly with us. We are in the middle of its life and movement. We pause for the courage to live the remaining day with integrity and faithfulness, and with a thought for other's needs.

None

We get our word "noon" from this afternoon hour which, at one time, was set back three hours.[11] But we shall stay with the original pattern and celebrate the hour of None, or Nones, as it is sometimes called, at its traditional afternoon time. "None," by the way, rhymes with "stone," and is pronouned exactly as we pronounce "known."[12]

The hour of None is the time of closing down and turning inward. It is midafternoon. You pause to look at the clock, thinking that you have just so much time left to do what you must do before the workday ends. Or you may have already passed this point and now be making the evening commute home. If it is winter, the sky is darkening; if summer, there is much of the hot day left. Thoughts turn to what has happened during the day; there have been some mistakes and there have also been moments of reward. This is a time for taking stock. The first task is to flush out all the worry and regret. Deal as well with it as you can. Acknowledge what went wrong and what your part in it may have been. If pain is carried over into the evening without examination, it contaminates. Also remember the good moments. If you did well, if you achieved what you intended, you can have some humility about that, remembering that you are in debt to many others, but it is also important to enjoy your good feeling. Revel in it and give thanks to God for the joy.

Now is the time to let the busy day fade as you move into the evening schedule and the serenity that characterizes the hour of None. It is a meditative time, a time to reflect. It is the hour to recall that "this too shall pass." It is also a time to forgive and ask for forgiveness. You have been hurt, and now struggle with what response you can make to that injury. There are many ways to go: revenge, cowardice, saying "it didn't happen," or perhaps figuring out why anyone would do something like that. None reminds us that we are not alone in our struggle. We have invoked God's presence with us throughout the day; we have kept the hours. There is no reason to think God will abandon us now as we scan the day.

At the hour of None, we face our mortality and our daily limitations. We come to terms with things as they are. It is a good time. It is real life. The psalmist says that "Those of low estate are but a breath, those of high estate are a delusion" (62:9). Things are not as fatal as they now appear, and tomorrow will bring a new chance. Thinking about these things while in God's presence becomes deeply healing prayer.

Vespers and Compline

Time to call it a day. The enveloping darkness brings serenity and synthesis. In some communities the two evening hours of Vespers and Compline are combined. Vespers was traditionally the time after sunset, the time called "eventide" while Compline was the last prayer said before going to sleep. Vespers, the earlier of the two, was a time to light the lamps, close the door, and eat supper. We ourselves switch on the lights, open the refrigerator, make a few calls, and look at the TV guide.

If you are able to arrange any peace and quiet, Vespers can be a time for reading, praying, and meditating on thoughts of God. In some ways it resembles Lauds, and together, they are the contemplative bookends of the day. Some may use the prayer patterns of their faith traditions, such as the *Breviary*, the *Book of Common Prayer*, or patterns often found in hymnals of various denominations. An excellent source for such a format is two books edited by Rueben Job and Norman Shawchuck.[13] These books offer a brief worship sequence and include fairly short quotations from Christian writers who have something of value to say. I encourage you to look in the endnotes of this chapter for more information about them. Many people use one source for evening devotions and then change to another, just to keep fresh. If you like, make your own selections, perhaps including a psalm, the Lord's Prayer, or whatever you discover brings you into a deeper awareness of God.

One way to share the Vesper hour with those who are at your table is to say Aaron's benediction at the end of the meal. (It had never before occurred to me that prayer at table could be anything other than "the blessing.") Here are the familiar verses.

> The LORD bless you and keep you;
> the LORD make his face to shine upon you and be
>   gracious to you;

the LORD lift up his countenance upon you, and give you peace. (Numbers 6:24-26)

But the Vesper hour may be the most hectic of your day. If there are children in the house, if there are guests, if the laundry and supper must be done, if you have a work assignment due the next day, and three or four other things, all at the same time—no way! Choose instead, the hour of Compline, when you are just about to turn out the light. If your energy is depleted, and you are not at all up for a lengthy time of devotions, then shorten the time, but don't on any account completely skip it. We do what we can do, and being faithful counts for a lot. "Doing Compline" will keep you tethered to the source of your strength.

Settle yourself down, relaxing your body and closing your eyes. Allow yourself to know that God is with you and has been all the day. A friend of mine reports that her mother would say of this time, "I just stop and invite my soul." If you like, read or say from memory the *Phos hilaron*, the "O Gracious Light," found in most daily offices, and used as a candle lighting hymn since the very earliest times in both the Eastern and Western churches. In the fourth century, Basil the Great speaks of singing it. The prayer-hymn may be used at either Vespers or Compline, or in the combined hours. There is something quite wonderful in ending the day by saying what has been said for so long and by so many who love God. This history hallows the words.

O gracious Light,
pure brightness of the everliving Father in heaven,
O Jesus Christ, holy and blessed!

Now as we come to the setting of the sun,
and our eyes behold the vesper light,
we sing your praises O God: Father, Son, and Holy Spirit.

You are worthy at all times to be praised by happy voices,
O Son of God, O Giver of life,
and to be glorified through all the worlds.[14]

Peace is what these hours are about. The sacred times we observe during the daytime are the moments of peace that intersect a busy day, just as islands offer places of rest in an unquiet sea. Observing them, we let go of the day's blows and stresses. The quiet evening hours prepare us to make a transition to the night's rest, preparing us to begin with confidence the coming morning hour. The evening hours are not a mindless forgetting, but rather, a putting aside, trusting that God will care for us in darkness and again bring the light. We move from activity to rest to activity again, all in a consciousness that God is over us, alongside us, and in us. Our praying is cyclical and rhythmic. Rather than experiencing our existence as disjointed and unconnected, we feel a continuous flow as one hour is followed by the next.

What the Hours Are Not

First, keeping the hours is not an achievement. We are by nature and upbringing a competitive people, and likely to either "do the hours" so that we can say we did, or do them "better" than we did last month. The hours are for gently holding us in a remembrance of God's presence. They are not something that needs to be mastered, or graded, or boasted about. It is important to enjoy them and not fall into a compulsive rule-keeping which kills the spirit of easy companionship. I have a Jesuit friend who has warned me that following any pattern can become obsessive. He asked that I stress the importance of not counting how many hours are observed and for how long at a time. He has a lifetime of experience in observing religious disciplines, and I take him seriously. If it is not too irreverent to the reader, may I suggest the word "fun" in connection with this sort of continuous prayer? Although they do not mean exactly the same thing, I'm using the word fun as it is connected to *joy*. It is a beautiful thing to feel accompanied by God, at all times, during the entire day, and it *feels* like the deepest sort of fun. At the very least, let's agree to be more lighthearted than grim as we do the hours.

The hours are not for escape. This is the second thing we must know. Scott Peck began his first and most popular book with the sentence, "Life is difficult."[15] From that moment on, he has the reader's attention, merely by acknowledging the truth we all know. We so much wish for an island or a closet, a place where "all this will go away." Religious practice can easily become an escape, a denial of reality, and a place of reclusivity. Asceticism, which is the practice of religious disciplines, can be perverted and deformed into self-inflicted pain or utter deadening of the distressed mind.

Be careful that your engagement with this or any model for praying does not become a crutch that prevents you from true growth. The test of whether any spiritual discipline is a good one or not is whether it makes the practitioner more whole, more what they are intended by the Creator to be. If something is good, we can tell it by seeing that it helps us realize our full potential.

And third, the hours are not magic. We delude ourselves if we believe that keeping the hours, each one without fail, will some-how stop car wrecks, prevent disease, or generally operate as Superman in our behalf. It is true that a quiet spirit, one that is focused and not fragmented, does give us the attention we need to escape some dangers. I'm certain that I am more inclined to make the wrong move and say the wrong thing when my mind is not centered in the present, but instead is absorbed with some problem I imagine may come. But, we ask, would not thinking about God's presence be just as distracting? Actually, you will find that your practice of this spiritual discipline clears your mind, rather than muddies it, making you better able to see things realistically and in context. This effect may become evident to you within a matter of days.

I have been saying what the hours are not. I must add one other negative comment, and that is that almost all spiritual disciplines have become trendy. It has become religiously correct to "do something spiritual." We are much like chronic dieters. We try high protein, then high carbohydrates, then low calorie and herbal approaches, whatever happens to be the science of the moment. The spiritual "diet" we need is one that nourishes us and draws us to God. The only way we can know what works, is to try it. If it does "work," so to speak, we will not need to advertise or enlist converts. We will not feel the need to sell this latest technique. Jesus said, "By their fruits shall you know them." As with a diet, it will show.

Praying the Hours as Conversion

So much for what the hours are and are not. What will this daily discipline do for me, you may ask. Before we decide to positively invest in praying the hours, we will want to know what will be accomplished by such a radical change in our attention. Changing from our familiar way of diffused inattention to one of focused attention on God is no small commitment. What we are talking about here is not just a little addition to the day. It is a shift in life direction, a changed orientation, in a word, it is conversion.

In religious circles the popular use of the word "conversion" usually implies either joining oneself to a particular faith group, as in "He converted to the Catholic Church," or in the case of others may mean a sudden turn toward faith in God, so that one might hear, "She was converted in a revival meeting last summer." However, there is another way in which we may think of conversion: that gradual formation of will and thought that is accomplished again and again over a lifetime. This last way of defining conversion suggests that we may continue throughout life to increase our congruence with God. Our attention would be converted from one reference point to another, that is, from ourselves to God.

One of the meanings of the verb "convert" is to change from one state to another, from one purpose to another.[16] Consider how keeping the hours, daily, yearly, and over decades, would affect the entire existence of a person who prayed in this way. The effect of such a sustained and intentional companionship is too profound to calculate. A daily focus on God nourishes a disciple's continuing growth following such initial movements as affiliating with a faith group, or even experiencing a one-time change of heart. The New Testament Greek word for this change is *metanoia*, a radical shift in perception and being, in other words, a turning around.[17] Such a turnaround may occur suddenly or not, but it remains stunted and unfulfilled if it is not *attended*.

Praying the hours is one way of attending to relationship with The Holy and engaging in continual conversion. As we have seen, stopping from time to time to reference God is not so much an addition of duties or of committing more time as it is a new way to see what it is that we are already doing. It is a way to see that all is holy, and that God is in all things. Psychologist Carl Jung had the phrase *Vocatus atque non vocatus deus aderit* carved above the front door of his house in Zurich; it was also on his tombstone. "Bidden or not bidden, God is present."[18] It is all a matter of seeing things as they actually are.

The habit of seeing God in every event and in each part of creation prepares us for the years ahead when age takes away stamina and perhaps health. Our culture focuses on the losses that later life brings, but never on its gains. We don't seem to know that the confinements of age set us free, sometimes for the first time in our lives, to attend to a rich inner life. Our fundamental assumption is that the good life is possible only to those who have near perfect health. We laud the eighty-year-old who attempts the comb of Mt. Everest, but pay no attention at all to the person who has undertaken to pray for the world and its ills. The key to a rich later life resides in the groundwork laid in the years that precede it. Praying the hours over many years grounds us in a familiarity with the presence of God that does not leave us, rather, it grows. It is an acquired skill and the best preparation we can make.

So what is next? Well, what time of day is it now, as you read? The next canonical hour is waiting. This framework of prayer pauses invites you to enter the stream of continuous remembrance of what is real: God's being with you and in you. The word "enjoy" comes to mind and suggests what can happen. You will enter a companionship that causes you to be in joy. This commonest of days is a sacrament of God, the visible form of invisible grace.

✤ VIGILS

Observed by those who are awake at night. Use the darkness simply to be with God, aware of the Holy Presence in your quiet hours. Prayers can be simple.

✤ LAUDS

Wake to thank and praise *(laudate)* God. This is the hour to spend some time in prayer and contemplation. Spend twenty minutes if you can.

✤ PRIME

Take just a moment to look over your day's calender, asking God to be in all you attempt to do.

✤ TERCE

Midmorning is break time. Deeply breathe in God's spirit before returning to your morning's tasks.

✤ SEXT

It is now noon and time to consider the whole world and its needs.

✤ NONE

In the afternoon we close down our work and turn toward home. It is a time for forgiving, asking forgiveness from God, and letting go of the day's events.

✤ VESPERS / COMPLINE

Close the day with peacefulness, prayer, and perhaps a bit of bedtime reading. Entrust your life to God until you greet the morning again with thanksgiving.

CHAPTER FOUR

Anchors

In 1970 I wrote of a "post-traditional world."
Today I believe that only living traditions
make it possible to have a world at all.
                              —Robert N. Bellah

Liberation theologian Leonardo Boff has written about the sacramental objects that bring connection to his life: his family's tin cup, a freshly baked loaf of bread, a memento from his father. He interprets these things as symbols anchoring him to his family. Wherever he travels in the world, the thought or sight of these objects becomes for him a lifeline to home. The objects have no power in themselves, but because they evoke strong associations of family life, they are for him sacramental objects, conveying familial love and closeness. He again participates as a family member by maintaining his connection to the family.

Boff believes that to live is to read and interpret. If we will but open our eyes, he writes, we'll be able to see that "the world [is] a great and grand sacrament of God" and that "all reality is but a sign."[1] He grieves that Christians have become dead to the meaning of the Church's sacramental moments, such as Baptism and Communion, and sees a process of what he calls "ritual mummification." If we are dead to God around us in the daily, why should we be moved toward God on special occasions? We may simply "feel religious" at such special moments but have little experience of what we earlier called the primary text.

Boff's story explains how it is that he is anchored both internally and externally. Certain things, such as the tin cup and the bread, trigger a response in him, and he then feels back in touch (anchored) to family. He comments on the sacramental life of the larger family, the Church, and regrets that these acts no longer have the power for many people that he finds in them for himself. The external act is meant to produce the internal response of being one with God and the community. Boff observes that for many there is no link.

Anchors Around Us

In the previous chapter we explored living each day in God's presence by observing the monastic hours. In this way, the day becomes a sacrament because of its lived out companionship. This kind of daily remembrance is an anchor for us, one that tethers us to God. It is a type of daily holiness embedded in common events. But there are other anchors that convey grace, other moments when we feel the Creator creating within us. Many such moments occur when we worship in community. While observing the hours in an interior, personal, and solitary practice, corporate worship provides the essential balance for a full spirituality. More important, it is good that God be worshiped by the believing community. The first among the Ten Commandments enjoins us not to worship other gods, but to worship the Lord our God above all else. This command involves every aspect of our lives, personal and corporate. We bring health and balance to life by engaging in both private and public worship.

The Church

Harvey Cox writes we are "more essentially religious than many of us have assumed. [We] thirst for mystery, meaning, community and even for some sort of ritual."[2] We may deny this pull toward the holy, but it is still there and, if not given expression, evidences itself in underground ways. We will do lots of weird things in order to feel the religious. Teilhard de Chardin expressed it as "the need to adore."[3]

Many feel disenchanted with the Church. Others have not been a part of church life enough to be disenchanted but may better be described as detached. The detached are often the children of the disenchanted. It is important to concede, at the outset, that the church has disappointed many and has proved itself capable of perpetrating genuine evil. That is difficult to say, but we know it is true. The church is composed of "us," and we ourselves are imperfect and so can be the cause of things truly evil. With that acknowledged, it is also true that the church is a sacrament in that it seeks to make known to us the presence of God, however imperfectly it goes about that task.

Think carefully about each act in a service of worship. We sing, and if we allow our minds and spirits to enter into the words and sounds, we experience what the song is about. We pray aloud in the worship service. In our private prayer, the conversation with God is done from our personal perspective. In corporate prayer, we hear the requests and praises voiced by many, and our perspective is changed. We are, in other words, enlarged. Private devotion is essential, but so is the corporate expression of devotion to God. Social observer, Robert Wuthnow, points to the fact that in contemporary culture "most pray for themselves rather than seeking to worship through their prayers."[4] Prayer is done both for ourselves and for God. The experience of worship in community is not better than or inferior to private devotion. Rather, each is different and brings its unique gift, one which no other form of expression can do.

Standing, sitting, kneeling, bowing, all these gestures, if paid attention to, are expressive of devotion. Hearing scripture read to us by another voice, and interpreted as to its meaning for us personally and as a society, is education in holiness. We hear the scripture text as being expressive of God, enabling us to know more about what God wants and gives. Especially profound for the Christian is Communion, what some call the Lord's Supper and others the Eucharist. This ceremony celebrates and remembers the life of Jesus and invites the worshiper to physically join in those events. There are probably as many beliefs about the bread and the wine as there are communicants at the altar. All of these interpretations have one thing in common. When participated in deeply and thoughtfully, Communion is transformative.

It was thought by primitive peoples that the ingesting of a particular animal would endow the one who ate with characteristics of the animal: bravery, strength, beauty, and so forth. When one eats bread and drinks wine as a representation of Jesus' death, one has the sense of becoming more like him, of moving from self-absorption toward sacrificial love. There are other important theological meanings connected to Communion, but eating, itself, is experienced by us as "becoming." The corporate experience is that we do this together, and we become what the church is called: the Body of Christ. We become what nourishes us, however one thinks that happens. A writer in the field of spirituality, Benedict J. Groeschel, offers this definition of the Eucharist. "It is," he says, "not a symbol, myth, or even memory, but a participation, through the Holy Spirit. . . ."[5] Groeschel's shift in emphasis is worth attention.

Participation in these corporate actions are what is meant by the term "spiritual formation." We are formed, again and again, by our regular participation in these acts. On a few occasions a one-time participation can be powerfully life changing for someone. What is fundamentally transformative, however, is the continuous and regular engagement in these acts and gestures. "Such habits help to shape the unconscious," says author, David Ford, "those layers of self where the sediment of the past is deposited and that nourish (or pollute) our instinct, intuitions, and reactions."[6] The Church becomes the powerful and solid anchor which holds us as we negotiate our lives. There are few anchors as binding, and few as able to tether us when the seas are rough. The community itself is teacher, safeguard, and solace. It is the well when we are dry and comfort when we grieve. It bridges between the good times and the bad, always there, continuously remembering and reminding.

Without a faith tradition, we must negotiate our spirituality each time we seek to worship. This renegotiation is not entirely a bad thing. It is possible that we may experience growth through remaking our understandings and experiences of the sacred. Nevertheless, says Wuthnow, this "results in a transient spiritual existence characterized more often by dabbling than by depth."[7] If both these ideas are true, that we grow both by flexibility and by rootedness, then it would seem that a balance is called for. On the one hand, we may discard the mindless following of unexamined teachings while, at the same time, allowing ourselves to tap into that rich reservoir of accumulated faith that was preserved and is now offered to us as grounding for our spiritual practice. We need not walk away from inquiry and new ways of approaching God. We do ourselves a great service, however, by going deeply into our chosen faith tradition and appropriating its gathered wisdom. Will our choice of a tradition lead us to the perfect church? No, it will not. Like our biological family, the church is flawed, but it is ours.

Groups of Us

Small groups committed to study or support can be anchors for spiritual life, especially those groups meeting together over a sustained period of time. The most effective groups seem to be those in which the truth can be told without fear of a judgmental response. This is one reason the varieties of Twelve Step groups flourish. Another kind of anchoring experience is the occasional retreat, workshop, or seminar which gives us the spiritual push we have been needing in order to move toward God in a new or deeper way. Something in us has been waiting and building, and perhaps the intensity of the group experience opens us to that new growth which, until now, has only been potential. We call it a "breakthrough" since it feels to us as though some truth has broken through to change us.

The Anchored Mind

In an instant-gratification society, we sometimes prefer the emotional moment to the long-term work of study. In truth, many who would be interested in the study of scripture and theology do not believe that they have the skills necessary to deal with these subjects. We listen to sermons (of mixed quality) in order to receive from someone else's study the second- or third-hand truth of the matter.

The Language of Scripture

One of the great gifts of Reformed spirituality to Christendom was the reclaiming of scripture for use by everyone. This access was worth fighting for, but, amazingly, we often slip back into turning scripture over to the scholars and church professionals. The result is that, through lack of engagement with them, we find ourselves no longer interested in the biblical texts.

So laziness is one problem. Ignorance is another. Should we decide we would like to become familiar with the scripture's revelation, the scholars and experts can be of enormous value to us. If we listen and learn from them, they will teach us to read with a trained eye and a critical mind. We will be able to take into consideration the history and culture of the times in which scripture texts were written and stop ourselves before accepting uninformed statements about what a passage does or doesn't say. There are scores of people for whom scripture has been con- taminated by the careless scholarship of so-called authorities. These people are bitter at the harm done to them and have quit the Church, or at the very least, have stopped listening to scrip- ture when it is read. The result is a growing disconnection between present values and our religious history.

For several years I worked as a therapist in a Samaritan coun- seling center. These are places where a client may hope to find competent professional psychotherapy plus a religious orienta- tion on the part of the counselor. Although some who came to us described themselves as nonreligious, most were people who had some connection to denominational church life. During my first two or three years there, I made the mistake of assuming that these church-connected clients knew the more familiar Bible stories. I was talking to a young woman whose previously married husband had just brought home a ten-year-old boy with the announcement, "He will be living with us, now." During previous visits she had told me of her unfulfilled longing for a child, and then came this all too sudden appearance of her new "son." Trying to quiet her fears and open up the possibilities of what had happened, I quoted to her the words of Mordecai to Esther, "And who knows whether you have not come into the kingdom for such a time as this?" (Esther 4:14 RSV). I hoped, by using such a line from this colorful story, to evoke for her Esther's changed and challenging destiny. My client's response was one of total silence and a puzzled, almost blank, expression. Who was Esther? she wondered. She could not imagine what I was talking about.

Working with other clients, I later tried New Testament parables, hoping for a sign of recognition and often found the same nonexpression on people's faces. I realized, finally, that these clients and I had lost a common language, a mutual point of reference that might have been not only a therapeutic shortcut, but a pathway toward cultural and moral insight. The stories and the teachings that come from scripture are a part of our spiritual legacy, our message in a bottle, so to speak, from God. They anchor childhood imaginations with vivid accounts about what works and what does not. They support us in our adult struggles to set priorities and pursue the good. They are the archetypes for moral conduct in a civil society and the metaphors of our life events. We cripple ourselves when we decide not to know scripture and have as shared experience only TV sitcoms and current movie plots.

As you know by now, this book is not about Bible study and how to go about it. There are many other books which cover that subject very effectively. But it is important to say that if we enter the twenty-first century without an anchor, a text, a rule of life, and a way to spiritually sustain ourselves, we will find ourselves adrift and lost. A Rule of Life for the twenty-first century must include in it somewhere, somehow, the reading and study of our common record of faith. You may want to do this privately, choosing books by authors you trust to guide you in your reading of scripture, or you may choose to join a Bible study group, and there are many. You may even admit that you dread this and feel little attraction to what seems to you either boring or punitive. Remember that there are perfectly well-adjusted people out there who are fascinated, even passionate, about this kind of inquiry. Seek them out. Avoid what feels dead or toxic and find a mentor who truly loves the study of scripture.

Reflective Reading

There is another kind of study which is called by one author "formative reading," a particularly apt term.[8] Actually, this is not study so much as it is a leisurely, reflective sort of reading. It is the kind of reading one does when he or she picks up a book written by a writer experienced in the spiritual life and savors short passages, read slowly. There is no effort here to master a body of information. The mood is more one of receptivity. The reader is waiting to see what might come to mind as a result of the reading. (When scripture itself is read in this way, it is called *lectio divina*, and you can learn more about this rich Benedictine practice through several authors.[9]) Find a bookstore or library that carries titles and authors you like and keep a book on the table beside you all the time. If you can't think what to buy, ask for suggestions from a friend who keeps up with this kind of reading or consult a favorite book's endnotes for ideas. I have made such a list, in a previous book,[10] as have others.[11] Meditative reading is ideal as a part of the observance of the longer "hours," presented in the previous chapter. Morning or evening are good times or whenever you have a bit of time to reflect on a passage after reading it. The secretary in my office keeps a book in her desk and reads short bits during lunch. It is her island in the day, a time when she reorients herself to God (if I don't intrude).

Visual Cues of the Holy

Some people like to see or feel some object which they regard as religious. Others are very much opposed to such things and what they fear is the temptation to idolatry. I'm talking about the wearing of crosses, the use of icons and other pictures, statues, Bibles, and any objects thought to be religious in nature. Such visual cues can indeed become the objects of our worship, rather than the God of whom they are meant to be reminders. Crossing over the line from the reverence of things to worshiping them is fairly easy to do, especially in times of personal stress. However, objects we use to enhance our remembrance of God can be profoundly affecting, helping to sharpen contemplative focus. Religious objects can be good or they can be bad, beneficial and destructive, depending on the power we invest in them. If we use them as doors to recollection, they are good for us. If we expect magic, or believe the object to be a talisman with creative power, we are misled and, eventually, disappointed.

When your cross, picture, Bible, or other object is an invitation to you to think of being in and with God, you have found a spiritual anchor. I know of few people who, after going on a particularly meaningful spiritual retreat, would not think of coming home without a special rock. It may be that as they took a walk in the woods, or down a rough, winding road, they experienced God's presence. All of us wish to extend and preserve such moments, so we pick up a leaf or a shell, some memento to remind us of what has occurred.

I have on my office desk a rock I retrieved while on a seven-day silent retreat in the hill country in Texas. It is actually two rock formations bonded together. The outer layer is dark and smooth and its cavity is filled with the light limestone sediment characteristic of that area. Sometimes, when I look at it I think of how, like the rock, God surrounds me. At other times I'm sure God is within, just as the sediment inhabits the stone. You could think of it as God's immanence and transcendence, I suppose, but mostly it brings back to me the experience I had during the retreat, that of being accompanied, although no other human being was there. The rock is an anchor for me. I do not ask the rock to make my life magically better, nor do I invoke its blessing. The blessing comes when I remember what it represents: God around me; God in me. I remember the "primary text."

We have been noticing those exterior things that are sacraments of God's presence with us, and in this context, have called them anchors. They are the things that cue our five senses, evoking their associated thoughts. They draw our attention toward the Holy One. When I see an altar or a sunset, I think worshipful thoughts and am filled with awe. If I rub my fingers over my hill country rock, I feel accompanied. The taste of red wine evokes memories of both dinner parties with friends and the communion rail and transformation; the smell of incense or of candles recalls high worship moments as well as visits to the neighboring Catholic church. Is it the rolling sound of an organ or is it the thrum of a guitar that makes you hum the hymn? Spiritual director Margaret Guenther writes of one woman who said she prays the Connecticut Turnpike. "I use the toll booths as markers, like the beads on a rosary," she said.[12] Indeed, all creation can become a sacramental anchor, letting us see the extraordinary within the ordinary. Albert Einstein observed that there are two ways that we may live our lives. One is that there are no miracles; the other that everything is a miracle. We are sensory beings, and God is speaking to us all the time and everywhere. These are the external cues. The internal task is to notice them.

Anchors Within

We have been learning a lot from Buddhism lately, and about what is called *mindfulness*. What we may not have realized is that all the great religions, including Christianity, have some version of this "being in the moment" teaching. What do we suppose Jesus meant when he advocated that we should "not be anxious for tomorrow, for tomorrow will care for itself" (Matthew 6:34 NASB)? One writer states it simply: "Mindfulness is to be aware of what is going on."[13] Much more easily said than done, especially for Westerners! Jesus was a man of the East and not particularly driven by our Western preoccupation with the clock or by the outward marks of success. Reading the Gospels, we see someone who does not obsessively worry about his future, which he surely had reason to do. He accepts what he suspects will happen and turns to the present moment, knowing it is there that he can fulfill himself and do his work. It is also in the present moment that he finds both his "brother" and "the Father."

Living in the Moment

God is found in the present. We have thoughts of the past, of course, but if we reflect on them, we realize that what we are thinking of is no longer happening. In reality we are having present-moment experiences that are simply memories. We worry over the future, though it doesn't yet exist. These are thoughts, not of memory, but of our present-moment imagination. We live in the present moment with both our memories and our imaginations. But the present is where we *always are*. Ideas such as these suggest the importance of being, as the spiritual masters say, "present to the moment." Actually, becoming conscious of the present moment in which we find ourselves is the anchor that holds us in reality. How often do we drive a car, have a conversation on the telephone, speak to a child, or attend a service of worship, all the while thinking of something else? While appearing to be present, we plan the future that does not exist. Or our thoughts dwell, not here, but on other similar moments, now long gone. It is one of the characteristics of modern life that we "jump ahead" in our minds. We are seldom *here*.

A Rule of Life that enables us to stay connected to God, to recognize God's immediate presence, would necessarily call for us to pay attention to what is happening now. How can we notice God's presence in the now if we are not present to that moment ourselves? This question does not suggest that the remembrance of divine care in the past is not helpful or good. The Hebrew Scriptures are full of admonitions to the Israelites to remember

God's past blessings. It is part of our present reality to remember. But that is not where we live. If we are to find God now, we must look for God now.

Do you recall the sacramental objects and acts cited earlier, those things that anchor our consciousness of God? If I would cultivate mindfulness and attention to the present, I must agree to allow those objects and circumstances to speak to me. If I am kneeling at the communion rail and thinking about lunch, how transforming do you think that moment will be? If I see a dramatic cloud formation and hear the drum roll of thunder but am thinking, all the while, about some past injury from a friend, how moved to awe will I become before this spectacle of nature? The external becomes sacrament only if it conveys grace to us internally. For grace to happen, something within us must respond to the grace that comes.

We are compelled by our experience to say that it is not possible to be consciously in the present at all times. We will never be able to perfectly achieve such a thing and should not expect to. We can, however, understand the value of being fully present and bend ourselves toward *noticing the now*, much more than we do. Just one example before we leave this idea: Have you ever been in conversation with someone and noticed that, as you are talking, they are already preparing what they will say to you, even before you are finished? At the very least, you do not feel heard when this happens. Under such circumstances your friend cannot, in fact, hear you. A mind that is busy crafting an answer is elsewhere. This is surely what God must experience when we are not present. God speaks in the moment. Holiness of life is the act of listening.

The Hasidic branch of Judaism sums up this belief by saying that redemption, like creation, takes place at every moment. Martin Buber writes that each moment we live is dialogue and that human beings find their purpose in "turning the whole of ... life in the world to God and then allowing it to open and unfold in all its moments until the last."[14] That dialogue with God, he says, is humankind's redemption.

Using "Triggers"

If you and I agree to a new framework for our thinking, we will see, as Einstein did, a miraculous universe in which all we encounter speaks to us of God. This change is not so much about adding disciplines to our already crowded lives. Rather, it is more about becoming *constantly conscious of God in what we are already doing*. We begin to see events and familiar objects in a revelatory light. What is meant here is not some spooky belief that we can interpret any subjective feeling we may have as God's voice telling us to do or not to do this or that. Just because we saw a black cat or heard some song on the car radio does not mean we are having direct instructions. There is already too much tendency to claim the endorsement of God on whatever it is we fancy at the moment. The sentence that begins with "God told me . . ." is to be spoken with caution. God does, indeed, speak to human beings. We know this happened to the biblical prophets and has happened to others since that time. Direct revelation of this sort, however, is rare and always for a good purpose. The "still, small voice" is much more common and is usually experienced as an inward prompting. Consciousness of God is simply that: being conscious of God's presence in and around us. This awareness creates a kind of hearing that allows God to speak in many ways. Our thoughts and actions are formed by this consciousness.

Our part is to remain available. It is God's initiative to speak, either directly, as to the prophets, or by permeating our lives, which is more typical to most of us. We do not choose how God speaks. Our choice is to listen to what is spoken, accepting it in the form in which it comes. One way to be available and conscious is to recognize what I call "triggers." The trigger on a machine or a weapon is the device that sets off the action. We often speak of certain events "triggering" other events. It is also true that what we experience can trigger an internal and spiritual response. Actually, we learn to associate what we experience with a thought or emotion.

Certain triggers can set off an association to thoughts of God's presence.

I have a favorite book about responding to the ordinary, daily events in our life in ways that will help us keep God in mind. *Being Home* by Gunilla Norris is full of examples of spiritual triggers. One of my students gave me a copy at the end of a course I taught. I noticed that the subtitle described it as a book of meditations, and I confess to having a certain dismissive attitude toward it. I am not attracted to what I think of as overly sentimental religion and am wary of sugary inspirational books. I suspected this to be one of those. It is anything but that. Norris makes a sacrament of the most ordinary household duties including making the bed, looking in the mirror, opening a window, taking out the trash, and my favorite, crossing a threshold. Of the last, she writes

Many times today I will cross over a threshold.
I hope to catch a few of those times.
I need to remember that my life is, in fact,
    a continuous series of thresholds:
from one moment to the next,
from one thought to the next,
from one action to the next.

Help me appreciate how awesome this is.
How many are the chances to be really alive . . .
to be aware of the enormous dimension
we live within.

On the threshold the entire past and the endless future
rush to meet one another.
They take hold of each other and laugh.
They are so happy to discover themselves
in the awareness of a human creature.
On the threshold the present breaks all boundaries.
It is a convergence,
a fellowship with all time and space.
We find You there.
And we are found by You there.

Help me cross into the present moment—
into wonder, into Your grace:
that "now-place," where we all are,
unfolding as Your life moment by moment.

Let me live on the threshold as threshold.[15]

There are so many things that trigger thoughts within us! When I see the photographs of my children on my desk, I think of them, and that prompts me to prayer for them and their families. I start my car or turn on my computer and, if I'm paying attention, am reminded that we all get a chance at new starts. It is my experience that God can bless just about anything, if we allow it. I have a low-grade fear of driving, so my car trips are saturated with thoughts of God's care of me. My clock chimes the hours, blessing me as it strikes, and reminds me that God has sustained my life up until this hour. I say the sound blesses me, but it does so only if I interpret the sound as a reminder of God, not just as a disconnected sound in the house.

Those of us who grew up saying "the blessing" before meals have an automatic and built-in trigger when we see food before us; we drop our head and are reminded to be grateful, whether we say a prayer or not. The gardener notices the dying seed and the growing sprout, and this sequence can bring to mind the constant creativity of God. The Hebrew prophet Isaiah rightly proclaimed that "the whole earth is full of [God's] glory" (6:3). Benedict emphasized the possibility of encounter with God at those times when we meet the stranger. "The stranger" may be any person, perhaps someone just introduced to you, or one very unlike you in appearance or background. This, said Benedict, is your chance to find God within that person. It is our choice to notice God in all creation or to deaden consciousness and ignore the message encased in the familiar.

Awareness of God and devotion to God is never achieved by crowding into the daily schedule yet another set of observances. It is more a matter of seeing the daily in another Light.

CHAPTER FIVE

Ways to Pray

Prayer is not so much our words to God as our life in God.

   —Unknown author quoted by Caroline Myss

In his first letter to his friends in Thessalonica, Paul advises that they should "rejoice always, *pray without ceasing*; and in everything give thanks" (5:16-18 NASB, italics mine). Muslims are told in the Koran to be in constant prayer, In order to keep their lives in perspective. On the face of it, these commands seem unreasonable. We know only too well that to be always forming the words of a prayer is an impossibility for us. We also know that we must go about our lives in a way that is responsible to our employer, our stockholders, our small children and older parents, and even to the government. We cannot afford to walk up against brick walls or amble out into traffic while mumbling prayers! However, our study thus far has shown that there are many ways of being connected to God including, but, as we will discuss further, not limited to, verbal prayers. We have thus far imagined several ways of adapting an intentionally spiritual life to fit twenty-first century living.

You may be thinking, "So many things to do! And now she is adding to the list other ways of praying? It's too much!" Actually, these are not so much lists of things for you to do, but, rather, pictures of a way of being. Some of what is presented here may suggest to you a sense of being accompanied by God. What if you are now beginning to see daily life from a different point of reference and in the light of a new Light? What if this way of seeing means that you believe one can continuously reference God as *here?* What this would mean, literally, is that one could be *constantly in prayer*, however that is done. If we define prayer as a lively awareness of God, not just words addressed to God, then cultivating this consciousness would be, as Paul says, to pray without ceasing.

"Prayer," says one author, "is primarily attentiveness to God's disclosure to us and the heart's response to that disclosure."[1] Later he asks, "What if our part in prayer is primarily letting God be given?"[2] If it is true that prayer is listening and response, and not primarily talking, then that drastically changes how we see prayer. If prayer is maintaining openness to and contact with God, then it is more an attitude than an activity. This openness would not eliminate our written and spoken "word prayers," but would include them in a much richer variety of ways in which we can relate to God. Nobody can say how many ways one can pray. There are as many ways as there are people, I would suppose. It is useful, however, to broaden our personal ideas of what praying can be. I have written previously on this subject in another book but would like to expand on it here, in the context of what we have been considering.[3] Praying is more than a list of requests to God, or statements about who God is, legitimate as those may be. Prayer is a relationship. As is true for any deeply held relationship, there are many levels of communication, not just one or two. True, we are encouraged by scripture to ask for what we need, but prayer includes more than making requests.

Word Prayers

Praying with words is our most familiar prayer style. We do much of our thinking with words; they are the tools whereby we manage our thoughts. The more words we know the more facile and nuanced will be our ability to process those thoughts. Since words are so important to those of us who have grown up in the West and have been educated in Western style, it is natural for us to pray using our most familiar mode: words. For many, the first prayer we ever prayed was taught to us as a word prayer, "Now I lay me down to sleep . . ."

Prayers We Write

If we attend what is sometimes called a "sacramental church," we are exposed to written prayers. Prayer books of every sort contain passages, some beautifully written, which have been said for centuries by faithful Christians. New liturgies and prayers are currently being written and revised, and changes in language keep the liturgy alive to contemporary ears. Gabriel O'Donnell and Robin Maas, in a chapter on liturgical prayer, believe that too often those who object to read or memorized prayers "are reacting out of the experience of having recited prayers without actually praying them."[4] It is true that such praying can be done without paying attention, just as it is true that extemporaneous prayer may be done as though on automatic pilot. It is not uncommon for those who typically do not use written prayers in their worship services to claim them for their private devotions. For them, the mixture of written and extemporaneous makes for a richer prayer life.

The *New Zealand Prayer Book* is written with English on the right-hand page and the Fijian, Tongan, and Maori languages on the left. The prayer for the Day of Pentecost (Whitsunday) is simple and makes a good beginning for any new day.

> God of power,
> may the boldness of your Spirit transform us,
> may the gentleness of your Spirit lead us,
> may the gifts of your Spirit
> be our goal and strength
> now and always.[5]

One of the Collects from this prayer book, the one for the third Sunday after Easter, serves as a greeting to the morning for New Zealand and Polynesian worshipers. It uses light as a metaphor for God.

God, you are the first light
cutting through the void.
You are the final light
Which we shall enjoy forever.
Help us to welcome the light and walk in it always.[6]

My favorite quotation about light is from T. S. Eliot's poem "Choruses from 'The Rock.' " It is the passage that begins

O Light Invisible, we praise Thee!
Too bright for mortal vision.
O Greater Light, we praise Thee for the less:
The eastern light our spires touch at morning,
The twilight over stagnant pools at batflight,
Moon light and star light, owl and moth light,
Glow-worm glowlight on a grassblade.
O Light Invisible, we worship Thee!

We thank Thee for the lights that we have kindled,
The light of altar and of sanctuary;
Small lights of those who meditate at midnight
And lights directed through the coloured panes of windows
And light reflected from the polished stone,
The gilded carven wood, the colored fresco.
Our gaze is submarine, our eyes look upward.
And see the light that fractures through unquiet water.
We see the light but see not whence it comes.
O Light Invisible, we glorify Thee![7]

The prayer poem goes on to describe manifestations of physical light which become reminders of the divine light. If you like Eliot, I recommend these lines as a deeply moving meditation.

Sometimes you will find a book containing collections of prayers, some of which are very good. One such book includes a prayer by James Martineau, especially helpful for putting one in a recollected frame of mind as the day unfolds.

Eternal God, who committest to us the swift and solemn trust of life; since we know not what a day may bring forth, but only that the hour for serving thee is always present, may we wake to the instant claims of thy holy will, not waiting for tomorrow, but yielding today. Consecrate with thy presence the way our feet may go, and the humblest work will shine, and the roughest place be made plain. Lift us above unrighteous anger and mistrust, into faith, and hope, and charity, by a simple and steadfast reliance on thy sure will. In all things draw us to the mind of Christ, that thy lost image may be traced again and thou mayest own us as at one with him and thee, to the glory of thy great name. Amen.[8]

Versions of the following prayer of confession dating from 1548 are still used by churches in the Anglican Communion, as well as other groups, and continue to meet the needs of people today. Heard most often on Sundays as a prayer of the congregation, it can also guide our thoughts as we end each weekday. Pray it slowly, thinking about each line.

> Most merciful God,
> we confess that we have sinned against thee
> in thought, word, and deed,
> by what we have done,
> and by what we have left undone.
> We have not loved thee with our whole heart;
> we have not loved our neighbors as ourselves.
> We are truly sorry and we humbly repent.
> For the sake of thy Son Jesus Christ,
> have mercy on us and forgive us;
> that we may delight in thy will,
> and walk in thy ways,
> to the glory of thy Name. Amen.[9]

Change the "thees" to "yous," and the "thys" to "yours," and you have the updated version.

There is something quite powerful in reading or hearing a prayer that perfectly, even elegantly, expresses one's inmost thoughts. Such prayers lift us and we find ourselves saying, "That is exactly what I mean!" The time-worn words are what we intend and are said the way we'd like to say them. At other times, what we hear in the prayers stretches us to pray for things we had not before considered. There is a vital place for the written words of prayers, carefully crafted and reverently said over time. The saying and hearing of them contributes in a significant way to what we call our "spiritual formation." They become embedded in mind and body.

Prayers for the Moment

Equally powerful are those spontaneous word-prayers, written and silent, which we personally make to God, as well as those made by one who speaks for the gathered group. At its best, extemporaneous prayer is conversation. If what we do is authentic, we are talking to God and not to each other. The point of such prayer is to express verbally what most concerns us. There are times we need to confess, putting into words what we know to be our part in wrongdoing. At other times we feel the need to express our love, praise, or gratitude. A mute heart will not do. We want to say, silently or out loud, what we feel inwardly.

Those who pray publicly have the obligation of giving voice to the concerns of many, a somewhat daunting task. At times of grief, confusion, and celebration, a publicly expressed prayer that attends to the immediate needs of the community is a powerfully cohesive force binding hearts together in one intention. We remember times of national loss and recall, perhaps on television or from the pulpit, the voiced prayer of one who speaks for us all.

One person I know laughs and claims that her privately expressed word-prayers are her way of getting therapy, making available to her a way to express anxiety, loss, worries, joy, even humor. The key, of course, is that she takes the risk that someone hears her. Along with the psalmist, she says that "none of those who wait for Thee will be ashamed" (25:3 NASB). She is not embarrassed saying to God what she would say to no other. She believes she will be heard and helped and that God will not turn away. Those accustomed to worship using the unwritten, spontaneous prayer are fortunate in that they know how to have a conversation, at least their side of it, with an approachable God.

Journal Prayers

These are extemporaneous prayers one writes on paper. When you think about it, writing one's own prayers combines the best of both the formal written prayer and the spontaneous one. On the one hand, you can express your immediate concerns while, on the other, you give yourself time to sort through the words that best suit what you mean. The chief benefit of writing a prayer is that the very writing and reading of it validates and makes concrete the concerns expressed. We tend not to take our praying seriously, especially when we later forget what our prayers were about. A journal, or whatever written form you choose, goes a long way in preventing this.

Think of this kind of written prayer as addressing a letter to God. You'll find that what you have concealed from yourself, perhaps because it was too painful to bear, becomes clearer in the writing. We may easily fool others and ourselves, but it is more difficult to say to God what we know in our deepest self is not so. Two very fine writers on the subject of prayer have said that "the desire for prayer is the desire for a meeting with truth."[10] This is most particularly true for us when we write out our prayers. Writing down our God-conversations brings more truth into our lives. Another advantage of written prayer is that, as days and weeks pass, the journal serves as a record of what has occupied our minds and emotions. We see how situations have developed since we first prayed about them. From a distance we are able to see, as Gerald May puts it, that "suffering is often . . . the outer clothing of growth."[11] Writing, over time, helps us to interpret our lives.

Let me offer an important warning. Always keep your journal private. One hears of people who "accidentally" leave their personal diaries out where they can be read by someone to whom they are unable to speak candidly. That means that the journal is being written, not for themselves, but for that other person. A journal-prayer is one addressed to God, not to someone who may pick up the pages and make a judgment about the writer based on what is written there. So don't edit for even an imaginary, human reader. I personally think writing in longhand is the best, most intimate way of doing journal prayer. It is said that longhand writing is more likely to engage the right brain, that creative part of ourselves. I do know some people who use the computer, and I will say that for those who use a secure entry code, the computer is more private. If you use a book journal, place it in an unobtrusive place or, if you wish, in a locked place. Do whatever you need to do to keep yourself from editing for anyone but the one to whom your prayer is addressed. It will keep you more honest.

Praying the Psalms

"There are just no words for this!" We search for words when we're overwhelmed, when the standard sentence will not do. Look to the psalms! Words for *this* are almost always there. Praying with psalm texts is a very Benedictine thing to do. The medieval monks, some illiterate, prayed through all one hundred and fifty of them each and every week, so that the Psalms became their chief source for both mental and verbal prayer. Many modern monastics still maintain this schedule. It was Benedict's intention that the words would slowly permeate one's heart, and the Psalms would, with repetition, become the natural language of the soul.

If we worship in a church where the Psalms are said each Sunday, we are probably familiar with those that either praise God's greatness or comfort and encourage us personally. But if you look closely you'll notice that the single most significant category of prayer in the Psalms is not that of praise but of lament. There are about forty psalms in the collection that express either anger or complaint. That is about a third of the text. These anguished passages serve us well when we feel abused or forgotten. Growing up, we all have complaints and feel anger or sorrow. Sometimes we have not been allowed to express our feelings, or we just haven't found a voice within ourselves. The psalms of lament give us a language for our prayers. A good example is from Psalm 55:

> Give ear to my prayer, O God;
>> do not hide yourself from my supplication.
> Attend to me, and answer me;
>> I am troubled in my complaint.
> I am distraught by the noise of the enemy,
>> because of the clamor of the wicked. . . .
> My heart is in anguish within me,
>> the terrors of death have fallen upon me.
>
> (vv. 1, 2,-3a, 4)

Are you angry, even enraged, but hesitant to confess that to God? Let the psalmist do it for you: "O my God, make them [my enemy] like the whirling dust; like chaff before the wind. So pursue them with Thy tempest, and terrify them with Thy storm" (83:13, 15 NASB). Are you grieved? "The LORD is near to the brokenhearted, and saves those who are crushed in spirit" (34:18 NASB). Are you amazed with a sudden realization? "For with Thee is the fountain of life; in Thy light we see light" (36:9). The one who must wait for an answer can say with the psalmist "Rest in the LORD and wait patiently for Him; fret not yourself . . ." (37:7 *The Book of Common Prayer,* p. 633), and for the one who is in pain, the another translation puts it, "Be kind to me, God— I'm in deep, deep trouble again. I've cried my eyes out. I feel hollow inside" (31:9 *The Message*). But there are other words for us there also. As we become more conscious of the physical world and our need to care for a fragile planet, we might repeat with the psalmist the lovely hymn of praise found in Psalm 104:12-18. It begins "By the streams the birds of the air have their habitation; they sing among the branches." The Psalms richly express the full range of our passions. This is the reason they have become the backbone of meditations for monastic communities, corporate worship and private devotion.

Ann Jeffers writes that "the psalmist proposes an alternative view of reality," and that when we say the Psalms we then begin to understand the Creator as sustainer of the universe. That understanding offers us a chance, she says, "to reassess our position as one link in the chain of living."[13] The Psalms put us in our true place and furnish us with the language of the human spirit. The Spanish word *desahogarse* means to "unsuffocate oneself,"[14] which is what this language enables us to do. We breathe freely when we say and pray the Psalms. Those who journal their prayers will also agree with the psalmist who says "my tongue is the pen of a ready writer" (45:1 NASB).

Rhythmic Praying

I wanted to call this "Peripatetic Prayer" because it often has to do with walking, but I was persuaded by several friends not to do that. Calling it rhythmic prayer is just a way of saying that prayers can be phrases said over and over to the rhythm of our walking, our breathing, or any other repetitive thing we do. Another culture calls one type of repeated prayer a mantra. However you think of it, it is a pleasure to do and useful, especially in a busy life. Christianity and Judaism have a tradition of such praying, as do other religions. For Christians, the classic in this field is *The Way of a Pilgrim* written about 1869 by a Russian *starets* or holy man.[15] The anonymous writer recounts how he made his way, walking across Russia, saying over and over a single prayer phrase.[16] At the end of his journey he writes that he no longer needs to remember to say the phrase: he has become the prayer.

Many people jog for exercise. Some get on treadmills, and others like to walk the dog, stroll in a park, or saunter down a neighborhood street. When we are late to an appointment, our walking is more like running, and we may be breathlessly praying for mercy from those who will disapprove of our late arrival. In any case, we are a society that moves, motivated by either fitness or by hurry. There is a calm and restoring way to sanctify this kind of travel time.

Even people who use a wheelchair will discover that they are not as confined when they use the motion of the chair to pray rhythmically. Others, immobilized by illness, can use their breathing pattern to engage in repeated prayer phrases. Walking, sitting, or lying down, all of those who live, breathe; and praying to the rhythm of our breathing is inviting God's spirit to breathe within us.

Choose a phrase that has a rhythmic feel to it and say it as you stride along. We have already noticed how much the Psalms help in expressing inward feelings. Actually, many were written to be sung, and even in translation, the words read with a certain beat to them. Try the familiar opening line of the twenty-third Psalm, "The LORD is my shepherd, I shall not want." Another psalm phrase is "God is our refuge and strength, a . . . present help in trouble" (46:1 NASB). Or try a hymn text: "Amazing grace, how sweet the sound" or "Joyful, joyful, we adore thee, God of glory, Lord of love." You don't need to recall the entire passage or hymn text, only the one or two lines that go with your step.

In the place where I work, I walk perhaps six to eight times a day from my office to the administration building and back. Occasionally, rather than think of the worry I'm attending to, I walk to a peaceful, rhythmic prayer and arrive in much better shape than I might have done. Scripture promises that God will keep in "perfect peace" the mind that is fixed on God. This brief, rhythmic refocusing provides an anchor for my thoughts, and what I imagined was a crisis is now only one more thing to solve. I can then join with Lady Julian in saying, "All will be well, and every sort of thing will be well."[17]

Other Ways to Pray

We are so accustomed to praying in words that we don't imagine ourselves doing it any other way. But if we think about it, we realize that we often do communicate without words. Many married couples, as well as people who have close friendships, know that they can be sitting together wordlessly on a porch or driving in a car and "be together" without speaking. At such moments, information does not need to be exchanged for closeness to occur. We experience a warm feeling of recognition when we pick out the face in a crowd that is the one for whom we have been waiting. We are too far away to speak, but, even at a distance, the tie is established. It is important to point out that this kind of unspoken bond is built on many previous conversations and times of being together.

Friendship with God is exactly the same. After many visits and many conversations in which we express in words the deepest thoughts of our hearts, we may feel a desire to abandon words and just "be with." In time, one does come to what can be described as a comfortable relationship with God. This easiness is grounded in familiarity and the trust we have learned to have. It is then that we may turn away from words, at least for a while, and wish only, as the scripture phrases it, to "abide." The word "abiding" is a good one to use in describing praying without words.

Praying in Pictures

One of the ways we can "abide" is through the use of mental images. As already noted, we in the West are more prone to use words than pictures. Words are abstract symbols of some concrete person, thing, or attribute, and we use them when we want to communicate. If I say the word "green," you think of the color green and not red. But if I say to you "Imagine the color gliltch," no image comes to mind. It is the colors that are real, not the words that represent them. In order for "gliltch" to mean something, I will need to first show you that color. If you can remember what you saw, I can use the word again, and you will know exactly the color to which I'm referring. Words are a type of shorthand. I no longer need to produce the color if a word will make it appear as an image in your mind.

So when we pray, why not access the source? Why not sometimes visualize rather than word-speak? For instance, let us say that you are anxious and worried about someone who is close to you. The verbal way to pray would be to say to God in words how distressed you feel and then ask that your loved one feel God's presence with them. This is a perfectly good way to pray, although somewhat bereft of richness and detail. Imagine, instead, that you say nothing but instead visualize that person. You see the person as strong and accepting of God's blessing, perhaps a blessing that falls on him or her like a cloak or like rain. The mental image encompasses much more of what you wish: strength, calmness, blessing, perhaps even envisioning this person as transformed or relieved.

Because we are not accustomed to it, some think of this kind of praying as weird, spooky, and somehow not valid. Well, it would be all those things if we expected that we had, in creating the picture, cast some sort of spell. But what we are doing in visualizing is evoking the desire we have for this person's good. Creating mind pictures is what Ann and Barry Ulanov have called *primary speech*. Their premise is that "the language of primary-process thinking is not verbal. It comes in pictures and emotion-laden wishes and is private to ourselves, not really communicable, even though we share it."[18] Words, as useful as they are, are one step removed from the original thought. The primary impression is rendered in mental pictures.

During the time I worked as a therapist, I had as clients several hypertensive cardiac patients. They came to counseling in order to learn to calm themselves and relax enough to prevent a recurrence of their heart dysfunctions. In working with these people, I would begin by talking to them about the importance of relaxing. I would then ask them to close their eyes and breathe deeply, letting the tension ease out of their bodies. But no words I said were half as effective as asking them to imagine the most tranquil place they had ever been. Relaxed and with eyes closed, some "saw" a beach and heard the waves rolling in; one visualized being on a wind swept rock ledge in the New Mexico desert; and another imagined herself in a rocking chair on her grandmother's front porch. The moment these pictures came to their minds, shoulders dropped, breathing slowed, and their expressions became pleasantly calm. They remained mentally alert, in fact some reported their thinking was clearer due to the reduction in their anxiety. It's interesting that most relaxing images that people choose are located out-of-doors.

Things we see about us in the natural world furnish abundant images for praying. There is a wonderful children's book called *Grandad's Prayers of the Earth* in which a boy learns from his grandfather that everything on earth prays. The way that trees reach for the sky, says the old man, is one way nature praises and prays. The fragrance of a flower and the movements of the tall grass are prayer. All is prayer if we will recognize it. "Standing on a snowy woods on a winter day," he says, "and watching your breath become part of the breath of the world is a way to pray."[19] If you wonder how to teach a child—and yourself—something about ecology and prayer, making the reciprocal connection between the earth and the Creator can transform the natural world for both of you.

It is not difficult to see how one can pray using mental images. It is, in fact, almost too easy, and that is because it is so natural. We automatically think in images, whereas when using words, we have to work a little. If you would like to try this for yourself, first sit in a comfortable, quiet place, close your eyes, and focus on letting your body relax. (Tense people do not pray very deeply.) As you allow your breathing to slow, mentally go to that place of absolute tranquillity and safety that you alone can see. How is it that you imagine God to be there? Is God a breeze, a glow of light, the person of Jesus, or some other picture? God for you may be represented by the ocean, or as the painting on the ceiling of the Sistine Chapel. As long as the representation is loving toward you, you cannot be far off. From here on, there are no more directions, except to say that at this point you are no longer in charge of these images. You will not need to force the picture any further. Just be in the scene you see and wait in calmness. If you wish, you can ask a question or express a feeling. Be patient and let whatever happens, happen.

We are so task oriented in our society that we believe we must reach a goal or achieve a result with whatever we attempt. There is no result here except that you have arrived at your place with God. The goal has already been reached. Years ago there was a movie, starring Peter Sellers, called *Being There*. Well, that is what this kind of praying is about: being there, being with God.

We recalled the peaceful way in which some couples and friends can be together, with or without speaking. This is also possible with God when we pray with images. This peaceful practice is also a useful way to pray during the workday's observance of the hours. Often there is no time to formulate sentences and give deliberate attention to word prayers. But a picture is instantaneous! We can imagine healing and help for ourselves and anyone we see.

The Prayer of the Body

Although we are inclined to forget it, we are embodied creatures. As a child it was explained to me that those who "crossed themselves" as part of their worship were doing so because they were superstitious and somehow not as "advanced." When I later learned the custom of making the sign of the cross, I realized the profound effect it had on my attitude. Sometimes we do it in thoughtless, even superstitious ways but, when entered into devotionally, the gesture can be deeply affecting. This is certainly not a comment on whether one should or should not make the sign of the cross. We do what we are accustomed to do within our denominational framework. Rather, it is to say that what we do with our bodies during worship moments matters very much. On hearing "Let us pray," those who have bowed their heads and closed their eyes know that this automatic movement has an effect. The gesture itself calls on us to refocus our attention. By bowing the head, we foster feelings of reverence. In closing our eyes, we invite a movement from paying attention to what is outside ourselves to what is happening inside. Just as signing the cross or kneeling can be done unthinkingly, so, too, can bowing the head. Nonetheless, we must acknowledge that physical movements are formational.

In short, words and images are not the only way in which we address God; we pray with our bodies. How could we do otherwise since it is in our bodies that we have life? Putting aside those customary gestures which are common to some denominations and not to others, let us notice the profound ways in which what we do with our bodies affects our prayer. Prayer, whether in a public setting or a private place, is always influenced by whether we are calm or agitated. If we want to pray deeply, the first thing we do is quiet our bodies. Most of us automatically close our eyes, and if we know ourselves and what calms us, we slow our breathing. Just these two things alone can be enough to bring one into the awareness of God's presence. For many, kneeling by their bedside or before an altar is the most expressive way to commune with God. For others it is walking to some favorite outdoor place and physically taking in the sight and sound of the land. We think that by doing these things we are "getting ready to pray." But we are *already praying* as we do them, just by making the movements and assuming the postures of reverence and attention.

We admire the dancer who, by movement alone, shows us what awe and triumph look like and how despair and grief are expressed. We watch a movie heroine stand at the edge of a precipice, and lift triumphant arms up high. How wonderful, we think, and our spirits vicariously exult through hers. We ourselves are more circumspect, secretly believing that to make our own gestures is not showing proper control, or worse, is in bad taste. My guess is that most of us will not change very much from the habitual ways most familiar to us. It is important, however, to know that our minds and spirits are not separate from our bodies and that the maker of the body is, indeed, the Creator.

We worship with our total selves. One therapist, working with clients who have closed themselves off from feelings, says to them the following: "Take your time to feel how this lives in your body."[20] If we also take the time to notice, we will feel that our prayer lives in both mind and body. When a twelve-year-old girl was asked why she skipped all the way home from school, she said, "I'm just showing God that I like Fridays."

Centering Prayer

Centering prayer is currently much favored among those who seek the "something more" in spiritual life. It is an approach to contemplative prayer and is not a new way to pray, but an adaptation of an ancient prayer discipline. Centering prayer will remind you of the previous discussion on how to pray with images, which is praying without words. The significant difference in centering prayer is that it is done, as much as possible, *without* images or mental pictures. This is true, contemplative prayer. It is called centering prayer because it brings us from the periphery to the center, that is, we learn to edit out all the static around us, including our worries, and focus on one thing. We focus on the still point within us where we can consciously join with God. It is much like being in the silence between sentences and the pause between notes. Poet Rainer Maria Rilke said "The problem is not whether the song will continue, but whether a dark space can be found where the notes can resonate."[21] True silence invites depth of spirit. Those who think that Western religions have only a tradition of meditation and do not have a contemplative way to pray are mistaken.

In meditation, we focus on an idea, a passage of scripture or a saying, or possibly gaze at an object. Our thoughts are gathered into the thing or idea we have chosen as our object for meditation. Meditation is both thoughtful and focused. Contemplation, however, though just as inward and wordless, is the practice of having no thoughts or concerns at all, as much as that is possible. Thomas Keating, one of its proponents, says "Centering prayer is an exercise in letting go."[22] You would think that just letting go would be the easiest thing in the world to do. Keating then quotes the Diamond Sutra which says "Try to develop a mind that does not cling to anything." Now this is very difficult! Our minds cling to everything. Sit quietly and try not to have thoughts. Every sort of picture comes before you, and you cannot imagine how you would turn it all off.

Freeing ourselves from our attachments is exactly the point of it. Because of our flighty minds and busy bodies, we are almost unable to be detached from our concerns, even for a few moments. As you may remember, we discovered that one of the common threads of teaching in the major world religions was the emphasis on detachment. Neither Eastern or Western religions have a corner on this concept. It is something thoughtful people have always known to be true. The more attached we are to outcomes and possessions, the less free and happy we are. Detachment, then, is caring less and less about events and "stuff," and more and more about orienting toward God. It is all a matter of attention. What is it that has your attention? Scripture says that whatever takes attention (allegiance) away from God is the idol we put in God's place. So would this mean that obsessive concern about these things could be the contemporary version of idolatry? Centering prayer suggests that it is and attempts to refocus the attention, shifting the fulcrum from self to God.

It is not possible in this short space to fully instruct readers in the discipline of centering prayer. There are retreat centers that teach this discipline. One good method is used by students at the seminary where I teach,[23] and there are many books that teach this technique. The Keating book mentioned above is a good place to begin. Read it through as an introduction and then follow the outline of instruction beginning on page 139. You need no equipment, only an open heart. What you will experience is safe and deeply restful. It is all a matter of trusting God to work in you while you rest in that wisdom.

Lectio Divina

Lectio divina is a category unto itself simply because it combines so much of what we have been considering as different ways to pray. Practiced as early as the sixth century, it is a discipline which is both verbal and mental, intentional and contemplative. The words are Latin, meaning "holy reading." Because of its appeal to so many temperaments, some people think of this approach as the ideal prayer form. One of the distinctive marks of Benedictine and Cistercian spirituality is the practice of praying with *lectio divina*.

As with centering prayer, the method cannot be fully presented in a short space; however, it is certainly possible to begin engaging in this way of "praying the scriptures" simply by following a few guidelines. The central focus in *lectio divina* is the passage of scripture chosen. Select a fairly short section of scripture, something you feel would be of value to you if you were to understand it more fully. The Psalms and the Gospel parables make good selections. The method involves reading the passage several times, each time approaching it in a different manner. Different teachers will present this approach in various ways, but the following format is one way that many like.

First, read through your selected passage of scripture without trying to "study" it, as we typically do. Just pay attention to what is written, noticing the detail that is in the story or the statements. This step is classically called *lectio* since it involves a simple but attentive reading.

The second reading is called *meditatio* because during this reading you meditate on the passage, thinking for the first time about what its meaning for you might be. Put yourself into the story or alongside the writer. This is a good time to play around with the ideas that come to you and spend some time with them. After an attentive reading followed by a meditative reading, *oratorio*, or prayer, can emerge. We naturally seek God as the scripture speaks to us, and our prayer is the response that rises out of what we have been thinking and feeling as we read the passage.

The final stage is called *contemplatio*, simply meaning a state of contemplation that we may experience as the last phase of such a subjective engagement with the passage. This is the stage most difficult for Westerners, as is centering prayer, because though it is so simple, it is yet unfamiliar. There is no goal or expectation here except to be in God's presence and in union with God. Do not be discouraged if this step is not easy for you. The first three steps are a wonderful way to pray, so follow the method as far as you are able. In time, the fourth step may come naturally.

There are several good books on the practice of *lectio divina*. In her book *The Practice of Prayer*, Margaret Guenther has three pages in which she beautifully summarizes this method of praying the scriptures.[24] There are also entire books written on this very effective approach to prayer.[25] I recommend *lectio divina* as being especially good for one's personal keeping of the evening hours of Vespers and Compline.

In summary, there are many ways to reach God, or, as we often say, to pray. The ones we have considered are these:

WORD PRAYERS	OTHER WAYS TO PRAY
written prayers	praying with mental pictures
extemporaneous prayers	
journal prayers	praying with the body
praying the psalms	centering prayer
rhythmic prayer	*lectio divina*

Prayer Is . . .

Author Caroline Myss quotes a friend who says "Authentic prayer does not mean to turn to God in order to get something; it means to turn to God in order to be with someone."[26] Exactly right! Prayer is neither a magic wand nor a dry duty. It is a relationship. To be conscious of God *is* to pray. The discovery of this extraordinary companionship with the Holy was central to the Rule of St. Benedict.

🌸 CHAPTER SIX

Facing Godward

We must be the change we wish to see in the world.
—Mahatma Gandhi

Former child actor, now director, Ron Howard, was interviewed in New York before an Actor's Studio audience of students. He was asked how it was that he learned his lines, even when he was a child too young to read. He answered that it was his father, also an actor, who taught him the skill. Howard's father told him not to worry about what he was to say next, but to focus his attention on what the other actor was saying and then respond to that. "When you listen to what is being said to you," remembered Howard, "then you know what comes next."[1]

Learning to Listen

The trouble with relating to God, it seems, is that we don't hear what God says. If, as has been claimed, God is everywhere, in everything, and is always speaking, then the problem may be with the *way* we are listening and not whether or not we are being spoken to. Teilhard de Chardin says "a Presence is never mute."[2] I rather suspect that we play a game of "I dare you" with God. Speak to me, God, in a way I cannot possibly miss, and if I hear you, then I'll answer. There is no little resentment in us about the scripture's admonition to pray, yet without giving us specific instructions about how that can be done.

115

Fourth-century theologian Gregory of Nyssa believed that sin is the failure to grow. We *can* grow in our ability to hear what is being said to us. By becoming conscious of the presence of God, who speaks to us in countless ways, we become listeners. Little by little, we can learn to "tune in" to the divine voice that is always speaking. Most of Jesus' parables said, in essence, that the divine presence is everywhere. In his story about the seed and the soils, the word that is spoken can fall on the fertile soil of our lives, not the barren, rocky parts. In my own life, my pre-occupation constitutes the rocky places. I'm thinking of every-thing except the moment that God is, in this moment, creating. The shallow soil of Jesus' parable is, for me, my distractions. I intend to be focused on the presence of the Holy One, but find that my attention is easily diverted by the most trivial things. My prayer begins in peacefulness, but often ends with the tension of imagining what will happen if I do not control the things that I picture. Like Ron Howard, we can only respond when we pay attention to what is being said to us. In order to do that, we must listen to the speaker. The French mystic Simone Weil wrote it well: "Attention is the only faculty of the soul that gives access to God."[3]

The *Opus Dei*

The Benedictines called their daily regime of prayer the *Opus Dei*, a Latin phrase meaning "the work of God." They believed that prayer was the chief work of their everyday life. We have been exploring the possibility that, living in times like our own, we might be able to create such a life of holy attention. Worldwatch speaks of "the acceleration of history" and of "the death of distance."[4] Our world is indescribably different from any preceding one. We find ourselves vastly more comfortable in body but often distressed in spirit. Do we have now all that there is, or is there something more? Is it possible to truly engage in a contemporary *Opus Dei?*

The *Opus Dei*, then as now, requires that we be present to each moment. That skill, that ability to be attentive to the *now*, is essential to what we have been describing as the recollected life. It supposes a life of always paying attention. Brother Lawrence, in his letters, talks about the "holy freedom" that he feels in his "familiarity with God" and observes that through attention, the presence of God becomes habitual in his daily life.[5] Our model for this undivided attention is the person of Jesus, and our goal is the one he articulated in his prayer, spoken on behalf of those present and those who were yet to come: ". . . that all of them may be one, Father, just as you are in me and I am in you" (John 17:21 NIV). This intertwining of the Creator and the creation is not simply a lofty idea. In Jesus, it became a lived reality, a way of facing Godward that he prayed would be true for everyone.

A Rule of Life is the schema we craft to accomplish a recollected life, one aimed at the intentional remembrance of God. It is the context for connectedness. This approach has worked for many others and boasts a long history of successful adaptation. The key is to see all things as holy and each day as a sacrament, that is, as the possible revealer of God's presence. If we want each day to be sacramental, we will arrange moments of remembrance throughout any given day. Benedict and others have observed the seven or eight "hours" that served to mark out all time as holy. We have seen what that might be like if practiced in our own time. We would begin and end the day with prayer, and possibly with some reading and meditation. The in-between times, however brief our prayers, can also be reminders of our continually being accompanied by God. In addition to "the hours," there are incidents and objects that we can enlist as "triggers," or associations, for prompting our devotional intention. In summary, we can be present to God and "always in prayer" simply by facing toward God with sustained attention. This continuing attention is fostered by our intentional crafting of moments of remembrance. This remembering is the *Opus Dei*, the work of God that we may carry out in any century and in all places.

Learning to See

Sometime last year, I saw written on a building the words, "The secret of discovery is not to seek new landscapes but to see them through new eyes." The recollected life is simply that, a new way of seeing and of being. In looking back over the many ways one could possibly draw into intimate friendship with God, we could easily be overwhelmed, thinking that all of it is just too much to "do." We review our present-day lives and know that we cannot add one more activity or responsibility to our already overextended schedules. But the recollected life is not so much about doing more things as it is about doing what we now do in a new way.

It was suggested, for example, that the midmorning hour of Terce, which was explained in chapter 3, could be a time for looking over the day's calendar, as we would have done anyway, a time for seeing the day in context of God's presence in our activities. The chapter about ways to pray suggested "walking prayers," which we called "rhythmic." These are the prayer phrases we can incorporate into walks we would already be taking on any normal day. Other occasions for seeing things differently may be as simple as crossing a threshold or sensing a change in weather. The first and last devotional observances in the day do take more of our time. They are the bookend moments at the beginning and end of the day in which we take ten or twenty minutes to calm ourselves, refresh, and rest in God's presence. On the whole, we are not so much adding time as revising the way time is seen. Walt Whitman writes about learning to see time differently.

> Why should I wish to see God better than this day?
> I see something of God each hour of the twenty-four, and each moment then,
> In the faces of men and women I see God, and in my own face in the glass.
> I find letters from God dropped in the street, and every one is signed by God's name.[6]

If we can't picture adopting all the hours at once, we can begin by choosing two or three, or even just one. Such a choice might become a portal to the other hours. No attention to God is ever wasted.

Resetting the Mind

Psychologist Robert Coles, writing in *The Secular Mind*, tells of trying to find out what theologian Paul Tillich meant by his use of the term "secular mind." Coles concludes, "I gathered, a secular person was one who looked within himself or herself, for whatever comprehension of the world is to be found, whereas the sacred mind looked toward the beyond, toward 'Another,' toward 'God.' " Coles here notes that we may shift our attention, as we might transfer our weight, from one orientation to another, thus setting a new direction.

Americans have learned to reset their clocks twice a year. When we do this, we are not actually adding or subtracting time, not in the long run, at least. But we are agreeing to see time differently for the next six months. Engaging in the *Opus Dei* is the resetting of our entire life in order to orient it toward another purpose—the work of God. It is not about additional duty but about a changed destination. It is a new way of being.

In the epigraph at the beginning of this chapter is a quotation from Mahatma Gandhi who writes that we must be the change we wish to see in the world. There is a wonderful myth in the Hebrew Kabbala which colorfully describes what it is we need to change, and where it is we need to go. In relating this story, Martin Buber tells of God who built and destroyed worlds and in so doing, caused sparks of light to fall. The sparks of light, which were parts of God, fell into each stone and plant—and also into human beings. It is the task of humankind, then, to "raise the holy spark," setting it free to return to its origin, which is God.[7] The image of the sparks, present in everything, echoes Benedict's teaching that all is holy.

In writing about the nature of humankind, Buber further declares that "the life of each creature is dialogue," suggesting that personal relationship with the Creator is, indeed, the human vocation.[8] He concludes by stating what he believes to be the ultimate human project. "Turning the whole of . . . life in the world to God and then allowing it to open and unfold in all its moments until the last—that is [our] work toward redemption."[9] That seems to be the summation of all we have been saying thus far: turning toward God, opening to blessing, and living moment by moment with full attention.

Yet it is even simpler than that. In the detail of our day, in the fine little minutiae of our hours, God has already blessed the interval between any two moments, and we need only still our frantic search and feel it. An appropriate concluding line comes from E. M. Forster's novel *Howard's End*, when one of the characters says "Only connect! That is the whole of [the] sermon."[10] Be still and know.

❧ Notes

Introduction

1. Kim Sue Lia Perkes, "More Christians Seeing Religion in a Different Light," *The Austin American-Statesman*, Sunday, December 12, 1999, sec. A, p. 10.

2. I am indebted to the Reverend Janne Alro Osborne for this interpretation, presented in her sermon at St. David's Episcopal Church, Austin, Texas, Summer 1999.

3. Hans Urs von Balthasar, *Prayer* (San Francisco: Ignatius Press, 1986).

4. Howard Thurman, *The Inward Journey* (New York: Harper and Bros., 1961).

5. Meister Eckhart as translated from the German by R. W. Southern, *Western Society and the Church in the Middle Ages*, *The Pelican History of the Church*, vol. 2 (Middlesex, England: Penguin Books, 1970–1985), p. 301.

6. Diane Ackerman, *Deep Play* (New York: Random House, 1999).

7. Ellen T. Charry, "Christian Spirituality: Whither?" *Theology Today* April, 1999, Vol. 56, No. 1, p. 1.

8. Robert Owens Scott, "From Super Ego to Higher Power," *Spirituality and Health*, Fall 1998, p. 1.

Chapter 1. Collected and Recollected

1. Geoffrey Wainwright, *Doxology: The Praise of God in Worship, Doctrine, and Life* (New York: Oxford University Press, 1980), ch. 11.

2. Paul Tillich, *Systematic Theology*, Vol. I (Chicago: The University of Chicago Press, 1951), pp. 53, 54.

3. Huston Smith, *The World's Religions* (New York: HarperSanFrancisco, 1991), p. 72.

4. Gerald G. May, M.D., *Addition and Grace: Love and Spirituality in the Healing of Addictions* (New York: Harper Collins, 1988), p. 92.

5. Quoted by Mary McAleese, "Approaching the Millennium," *Spirituality*, vol. 5, no. 24, June 1999, p. 132.

6. Patrick Heavey, "A Muslim Poet: An Introduction to Jalaluddin Rumi," *Spirituality*, vol. 5, no. 24, June 1999, p. 177.

7. Herman E. Schaalman, "Judaic Spirituality," *Chicago Studies*, April 1997, vol. 36, no. 1, p. 40.

8. Thomas Cahill, *The Gifts of the Jews* (New York: Doubleday, 1998), p. 249.

9. Edward Schillebeeckx, *Jesus: An Experiment in Christology* (New York: Seabury Press, 1979), pp. 652-53.

10. Dietrich Bonhoeffer, *The Cost of Discipleship* (New York: Macmillan, 1963), p. 7.

11. Psalm 31:5.

12. Smith, *The World's Religions*, p. 380.

Chapter 2. What Is a Rule?

1. For more on the *Amidah*, see Aryeh Kaplan, *Jewish Meditation: A Practical Guide* (New York: Schocken Books, 1985), chapters 11 and 12.

2. *Oxford American Dictionary*, Eugene Ehrlich, Stuart Berg Flexner, Gorton Carruth, Joyce M. Hawkins, eds. (New York: Avon Books, 1980), p. 734.

3. Benjamin Franklin, *The Autobiography* (New York: Vintage Books/The Library of America, 1990), p. 82.

4. Ibid., p. 85.

5. Stephen R. Covey, *The 7 Habits of Highly Effective People: Powerful Lessons in Personal Change* (New York: Simon & Schuster, 1989).

6. R. W. Southern, *Western Society and the Church in the Middle Ages*, The Pelican History of the Church, vol. 2 (Middlesex, England: Penguin Books Ltd., 1970–1985), p. 215.

7. *RS1980: The Rule of St. Benedict in English* (Collegeville, Minn.: The Liturgical Press, 1981).

8. Esther de Waal, *A Life-Giving Way: A Commentary on the Rule of St. Benedict* (Collegeville, Minn.: The Liturgical Press, 1995), p. xiv.

9. John E. Booty, *The Church in History* (New York: The Seabury Press, 1979), p. 93.

10. de Waal, *A Life-Giving Way*, p. 17.

11. Joan Chittister, *Wisdom Distilled From the Daily* (San Francisco: HarperSanFrancisco, 1991), p. 2.

12. Kathleen Norris, *The Cloister Walk* (New York: Riverhead Books, 1996).

13. Brother Lawrence, *The Practice of the Presence of God* (Old Tappan, N.J.: Fleming H. Revell, Spire Books), p. 17.

14. William Seth Adams, *Moving the Furniture: Liturgical Theory, Practice, and Environment* (New York: Church Publishing, 1999), p. 4.

Chapter 3. The Sacramental Day

1. Anthony de Mello, *Contact with God: Retreat Conferences* (Chicago: Loyola University Press, 1991), pp. 57, 58.

2. F. L. Cross and E. A. Livingstone, eds., *The Oxford Dictionary of the Christian Church* (New York: Oxford University Press, 1983), p. 1218.

3. Sincha Raz, *Hasidic Wisdom: Sayings from the Jewish Sages* (Northvale, N.J.: Jason Aronson, 1997), p. 19.

4. Robert Wuthnow, *After Heaven: Spirituality in America Since the 1950s* (Berkeley: University of California Press, 1998), p. 113.

5. Ibid.

6. Sandi Dolbee, "A Look Inside: The Me Generation Searches for Its Soul," *San Diego Union-Tribune*, 20 May 1994, E1.

7. John P. Harthan, *The Book of Hours* (New York: Thomas Y. Crowell, 1977), p. 11.

8. *Spiritual Traditions for the Contemporary Church*, Robin Maas and Gabriel O'Donnell, eds. (Nashville: Abingdon Press, 1990), p. 290.

9. *New Catholic Encyclopedia*, vol. 1, Catholic University of America (New York: McGraw-Hill, 1967–79), p. 521.

10. David Steindl-Rast with Sharon Lebell, *Music of Silence: A Sacred Journey Through the Hours of the Days* (Berkeley, Calif.: Seastone, 1989), pp. 76, 77.

11. G. J. Wuthnow, *Time in History* (New York: Oxford University Press, 1989), p. 108.

12. *The American Heritage Dictionary: Users Guide for Macintosh* (Novato, Calif.: WordStar International, 1993).

13. Rueben P. Job and Norman Shawchuck, eds. *A Guide to Prayer for Ministers and Other Servants* (Nashville: The Upper Room, 1983), and *A Guide to Prayer for All God's People* (Nashville: The Upper Room, 1990).

14. *The Book of Common Prayer* (New York: The Church Hymnal Corporation, 1979), p. 139.

15. M. Scott Peck, *The Road Less Traveled* (New York: Simon and Schuster, 1978), p. 15.

16. *The American Heritage Dictionary.*

17. *Vine's Expository Dictionary of New Testament Words* (Westwood, N.J.: Barbour, 1940), p. 280.

18. *Signals: Friends of Public Television*, Spring 2000, p. 34.

Chapter 4. Anchors

1. Leonardo Boff, *Sacraments of Life, Life of Sacraments* (Portland, Ore.: Pastoral Press, 1975), p. 2.

2. Harvey Cox , "For Christ's Sake," *Playboy*, January 1970. [as quoted by John Macquarrie, *Paths in Spirituality* (Ridgefield, Conn.: Morehouse, 1992), p. 3.

3. Pierre Teilhard de Chardin, *The Divine Milieu* (New York: Harper, 1960), p. 118.

4. Robert Wuthnow, *After Heaven: Spirituality in America Since the 1950s* (Berkeley: University of California Press, 1998), p. 7.

5. Benedict J. Groeschel, *Spiritual Passages: The Psychology of Spiritual Development* (New York: Crossroad, 1999), p. 29.

6. David F. Ford, *The Shape of Living: Spiritual Directions for Everyday Life* (Kentwood, Mich.: Baker Books, 1997), p. 113.

7. Wuthnow, *After Heaven*, p. 168.

8. Allan H. Sager, *Gospel-Centered Spirituality* (Minneapolis, Minn.: Fortress, 1990), p. 101.

9. Short explanations can be found in the following two books: Chester P. Michael and Marie C. Norrisey, *Prayer and Temperament: Different Prayer Forms for Different Personality Types* (Charlottesville, Vir: The Open Door, 1984), pp. 31-37, and Corinne Ware, *Discover Your Spiritual Type* (Bethesda, Md.: Alban Institute, 1995), pp. 101-07. A book length treatment: Martin L. Smith, *The Word Is Very Near You: A Guide to Praying with Scripture* (Cambridge, Mass.: Cowley, 1987).

10. Corinne Ware, *Connecting to God* (Bethesda, Md.: Alban Institute, 1997), chapter 5, beginning p. 49.

11. Sager, *Gospel-Centered Spirituality*, chapter 8, beginning p. 101.

12. Margaret Guenther, *Holy Listening: The Art of Spiritual Direction* (Cambridge, Mass.: Cowley, 1992), p. 20.

13. Thich Nhat Hanh, *Living Buddha, Living Christ* (New York: Putnam Riverhead Books, 1995), p. 110.

14. Martin Buber, *The Origin and Meaning of Hasidism* (New York: Horizon Press, 1960), p. 111.

15. Gunilla Norris, *Being Home: A Book of Meditations* (New York: Bell Tower, 1991), pp. 14, 15.

Chapter 5. Ways to Pray

1. Martin L. Smith, *The Word Is Very Near You: A Guide to Praying with Scripture* (Cambridge, Mass.: Cowley, 1989), p. 19.

2. Ibid.

3. Corinne Ware, *Connecting to God* (Bethesda, Maryland: The Alban Institute, 1997), pp. 31-48.

4. Robin Maas and Gabriel O'Donnell, "Prayer, Prayers, and Popular Devotion in Roman Catholicism" in *Spiritual Traditions for the Contemporary Church* (Nashville: Abingdon Press, 1990), p. 381.

5. *A New Zealand Prayer Book, He Karakia Mihinare o Aotearoa* (New York: HarperSanFrancisco, 1997), p. 541.

6. Ibid., p. 597.

7. T. S. Eliot, *The Complete Poems and Plays: 1909–1950* (New York: Harcourt, Brace & World, 1952), pp. 112, 113.

8. Quoted in *Minister's Prayer Book: An Order of Prayers and Readings,* John W. Doberstain, ed. (Philadelphia: Fortress Press, 1986), p. 51.

9. *The Book of Common Prayer* (New York: The Church Hymnal Corporation, 1979), p. 331.

10. Ann and Barry Ulanov, *Primary Speech: A Psychology of Prayer* (Atlanta: John Knox, 1982), p. 18.

11. Gerald G. May, *Care of Mind, Care of Spirit: Psychiatric Dimensions of Spiritual Direction* (San Francisco: Harper & Row, 1982), p. 50.

12. *The Message: The New Testament, Psalms, and Proverbs in Contemporary Language*, tr. Eugene H. Peterson (Colorado Springs: NavPress, 1995), p. 388.

13. Ann Jeffers, "The Earth Is Full of Your Creatures," in *The Spirituality of the Psalms, The Way Supplement 87*, Autumn 1996, p. 32.

14. Luis Alonzo Schökel, in "True Language of the Human Spirit," *The Spirituality of the Psalms, The Way Supplement 87*, Autumn 1996, p. 45.

15. *The Way of a Pilgrim* and *The Pilgrim Continues His Way*, trans. R. M. French (New York: Seabury, 1965).

16. "Lord, Jesus Christ, Son of God, have mercy on me, a sinner."

17. Julian of Norwich, *Showings* (New York: Paulist Press, 1978), p. 149.

18. Ulanov and Ulanov, *Primary Speech*, p. 3.

19. Douglas Wood, *Granddad's Prayers of the Earth* (Cambridge, Mass.: Candlewick Press, 1999), p. 17.

20. Mia Leijssen, "When the Client Is Too Far or Too Close to the Experience," *Psychotherapy Book News: A Journal of Essays and Reviews*, January 2, 2000, p. 25. Article excerpted from *Handbook of Experiential Psychotherapy*, ed. by Leslie S. Greenberg, Jeanne C. Watson, and Germain Lietaer (New York: The Guilford Press, 1998).

21. *Silver Departures: A Collection of Quotations*, compiler, Richard Kehl (La Jolla, Calif.: Green Tiger Press, 1983), p. 6.

22. Thomas Keating, *Open Mind, Open Heart: The Contemplative Dimension of the Gospel* (New York: Continuum, 1992), p. 74.

23. Alta Retreat Center, P.O. Box 407, Driggs, ID, 83422. Call (307) 353-8100 to speak to the Rev. Sandy Casey-Martus, Director. Alta Retreat Center is located in the Grand Teton mountains. Retreats are held year round.

24. Margaret Guenther, *The Practice of Prayer* (Cambridge, Mass.: Cowley, 1998), pp. 67-69.

25. M. Basil Pennington, *Lectio Divina: Renewing the Ancient Practice of Praying the Scriptures* (New York: Crossroad, 1998) and Martin L. Smith, *The Word Is Very Near You: A Guide to Praying with Scripture* (Cambridge, Mass.: Cowley, 1989).

26. Caroline Myss, *Anatomy of the Spirit: The Seven Stages of Power and Healing* (New York: Harmony Books, 1996), p. 282.

Chapter 6. Facing Godward

1. Interview with Ron Howard by James Lipton, "Inside the Actor's Studio," shown on C-Span 2, 1999.

2. Pierre Teilhard de Chardin, scribbled note found at his death, quoted by Thomas Cahill in *The Gifts of the Jews* (New York: Doubleday, 1998), p. 265.

3. Translated and quoted by Diogenes Allen, *Spiritual Theology: The Theology of Yesterday for Spiritual Help Today* (Cambridge, Mass.: Cowley, 1997), p. 82.

4. Quoted by Patrick D. Miller, "The State of the World," *Theology Today*, Vol. 56, No. 2, p. 148.

5. Brother Lawrence, *The Practice of the Presence of God* (Old Tappan, N.J.: Fleming H. Revell, Spire Books, 1977), p. 32.

6. *Walt Whitman's Leaves of Grass*, ed. Malcolm Cowley (New York: Penguin Books, 1959), p. 83.

7. Martin Buber, *The Origin and Meaning of Hasidism* (New York: Horizon Press, 1960), pp. 207, 208.

8. Ibid., p. 91.

9. Ibid., pp. 111, 112.

10. E. M. Forster, *Howard's End* (New York: Bantam Classics, 1985), p. 147.

🌹 Study Guide

1. Collected and Recollected

1. Do you think of yourself as a calm, even tranquil person or would you describe yourself as a bit frazzled and your life as somewhat hectic? How do other people see you on the calm-to-frazzled scale? If 1 is calm and 10 is frazzled, where are you on the scale?

2. Is there enough time in each day?

3. What measures do you take each day (week, month) to collect your thoughts and become centered in yourself and in God? Jot down the strategy that works best for you.

4. If you were perfectly honest with yourself, would you describe such quiet, reflective times as uncomfortable? If so, what is it about these moments that is frightening? Is there anything about them that is comforting?

5. Based on what you know of the Gospels, how would you describe Jesus on the calm-to-frazzled scale? What are the things you notice about his use of time? Can you remember instances when he is described as being quiet or prayerful? Was he ever upset?

2. What Is a Rule?

1. In chapter 1 the word "recollection" was defined as the concentration of the attention on the presence of God. Note below when it is that you most keenly feel God's presence with you or in you.

2. Does the word "rule" have a negative or restrictive sound to you? List below some rules that you dislike. How is a pattern of spiritual attention (a Rule of Life) any different from the rules imposed by government, work, schools, society, and family?

3. Why is it that a spiritual Rule can be helpful and liberating for one person and life-killing and punitive for another? What makes the difference?

4. Is there anything about the spiritual practices of those who have gone before us (the Desert Fathers, the monastic orders, and others) that you think might be helpful in your own life? Make some notes about those practices. Also note those practices which you feel are not relevant for today.

5. How important is ritual and repetition to your spiritual growth? What patterns of worship and devotion have affected you most? What would you subtract or add to any of these patterns in your own Rule?

🌹3. The Sacramental Day

1. Do you believe that it is possible to be "recollected" in the United States in the twenty-first century? If so, what changes would have to be made in one's personal life? In institutional church life?

2. Do you believe God "speaks" to human beings, or is God mostly hidden from us? If God speaks, what is the language used? Note the way in which you are most likely to "hear" God communicate with you.

3. Do you feel closest to God when you are in church among other worshiping Christians, when you are out in nature, or when you are alone? Can you say why these or any other settings foster this closeness?

4. Jot down an outline of your present daily or weekly devotional pattern. Include prayer times, reading that is spiritually nourishing, and any quiet times, such as walking or driving or pausing for a drink of water.

5. If you were to adapt the monastic hours to fit your own life, which ones would you include and which ones would you omit? What other changes would you make? Write an outline of your adapted use of The Hours.

4. Anchors

1. Some denominations have what are called "the sacraments." Based on what you learned in chapter 4, what is the broader meaning of the word sacrament? Write a definition that expresses what this means to you.

2. Leonardo Boff spoke of some sacramental objects in his life. Name some things, people, or places which have sacramental value for you. Of what do they remind you?

3. When your spiritual well runs dry, what things, person(s), place, or memory keeps you going? What "grounds" you and sees you through the difficult times?

4. Have you found any reading material that is spiritually nourishing to you? What books have affected you most? Is scripture reading part of what you like to do? If not, why do you suppose that is?

5. Have you ever just been going about your regular life and noticed something that caused you to feel God was intensely present? Describe some of these times of "mindfulness." How can these experiences become a habit?

5. Ways to Pray

1. Were we to be honest about it, many of us would say that prayer is difficult. List some reasons why prayer is a problem or struggle for you or for those you know.

2. Think about your church or faith group. What is typically thought of as prayer by that group? Are prayers usually said out loud, silently, together, privately, just at certain times? Make some notes about how your own notions of prayer are affected by your church and upbringing.

3. How does it feel when you pray in a new way? Has it ever seemed uncomfortable or even irreverent?

4. Review the various ways of praying explained in this chapter. What would you be willing to try that you have not tried before? Why does trying this new way of praying appeal to you?

5. Can a person pray using a scripture passage? Why do you suppose that is so effective for some people? Can a person sit in silence and still be praying? What do you suppose is happening while people are silent?

🌹 *6. Facing Godward*

1. Reread the epigraph which begins chapter 6. This quotation by Mahatma Gandhi asks the reader what change he or she wishes to see in the world. Write below the change you believe would most benefit humankind.

2. When you pray, do you think about the change you have noted above? What do you feel God is wanting of you to facilitate this change?

3. Part of the *Opus Dei*, that is, "the work of God," is simply paying attention. Is this too simple a thing (or too difficult) for people to do? Would it make any difference in the change you want in the world if you were to develop this habit?

4. Do you think having a contemporary Rule of Life is a good idea? Do you think such a Rule might help you better hear "the still, small voice of God" in the midst of the speed and sensory overload you are experiencing? Take time now to draft your own Rule of Life, knowing that you will probably need to revise it several times before you have found the patterns and practices that work best for you.